# Prerequisites to Ecstasy

*A No-Nonsense Guide to What It Really Takes to Create the Love and Sex We Say We Want*

## Om Rupani

## MAN - WOMAN

## FRIENDLY RELATING

# DESIRE

## SURRENDER

# About Om Rupani

**Me:**

This has been an unexpected journey. Over the past 10 years, any given week of my life has contained moments such as:

- Me leading a roomful of couples in the fine art of pussy-stroking. A room full of women on their backs, legs apart. Women being prompted to keep their hips relaxed and still. Women being prompted to stay present to the touch of their partners who are sitting astride them and with a soft contact, stroking their clits. I energetically feel into where the women are in their systems and guide the men in how to stroke them with greater acumen, when to slow down the stroke, when to speed up, when to stroke with a slightly greater emphasis on the upward rather than downward motion.

- Me counseling a couple who has come for a private coaching session seeking insight into what is keeping them from moving deeper in their relating and sexing; getting them to speak the truths they have been withholding from each other. Then taking them into my 'play-room' or 'dungeon-space' and guiding them in a scene with each other —which may involve any one of 100 scenarios. I might teach the guy how to secure his gal's wrist with some bondage rope, and then tie her up to a ring that is hanging above her head. Where can he go from there? He might proceed to relish her, or spank her, or... talk to her. Or I may guide the woman into stepping into her Dominant archetype, have her put on her stilettos and leather corset, have her put her man on his knees in front of her, have him bow down to her in a gesture of surrender while she digs her heels into his bare back.

- Training a class full of people over a weekend in the genial art of Dominance & Submission. Guiding them towards increasing their capacity for holding a generous and attentive space for their partners, so that their partner might feel invited to give up control and surrender. Teaching them safety and technique for rope bondage and impact play—spanking, flogging, caning, etc. Guiding them in designing good scenes that serve the desires of both parters. Encouraging them to speak their limits in real time.

- Co-teaching a class in Tantra & BDSM. Leading the students in an exercise of emotional release where participants lie on their backs and pound their fists into pillows and exhale with guttural sounds and try to let go of old stories and emotions that are holding them back.

- Doing a FaceTime call with a couple 3000 miles away and giving them the same guidance I give to couples in person. Guiding them through a D/S scene from across the country!

- Doing a spanking demo at a D/S convention where I'm teaching some workshops.

- Leading an online class in erotic writing.

- Having a group of actors explore how they can go deeper in to the archetypes of the characters they are playing by first exploring their own dominant and submissive archetypes.

- Teaching a men's workshop. Encouraging the boys to give up their preoccupation with techniques and routines and replace it with curiosity and attention.

**Not what I thought I'd be doing when I grew up!**

I had planned on a more sensible life. I'm Indian after all! Indian boys are supposed to be engineers and doctors. Bankers and coders. Indeed, I started school at Boston University as a Biomedical Engineer, with a side order of Pre-Medicine. I grew up in the common ethic of a typical first-generation, immigrant Indian household — we have come far! We made it to the U.S. of A. Land of opportunity. Work hard! Build a good and prosperous life. Good school is crucial for getting trained in some sensible money-making field. Be practical. Work hard and you can have it too—the American Dream.

Nobody sold me on this ethos. I was all for it. I was practical and sensible all on my own. Had grown up knowing I had a pretty good head — near the top of my class, teacher's pet, good at math and science. Engineering and Medicine felt like sensible choices.

I tried to make it work. I really wanted it all to work.

# Losing Track

Have you ever gotten lost on a hiking trail? You are moseying along on a lovely clear day, taking in the fresh air and the rocks and the sky and the desert flowers that have just serendipitously come into bloom because you are lucky enough to have shown up here to this otherwise barren landscape just a day or two after a rare rainfall. You are ambling along for a while and you notice that the trail has gotten a bit rougher than it was when you started. But you don't really think anything of it. You keep going, return your focus to this lovely outing and the air and the rocks and the sky. You return to your reverie, to how you don't get out enough to such communion with nature. The more you walk, the more light your mind seems to get. Things that had been nagging you all week or all month seem to release their tentacles from your brain. You feel a certain rejuvenation and primal lucidity coming into your thoughts. And then you notice that the trail really has gotten much more rugged than how it felt at the beginning — so much so that you are having a difficult time discerning what is the trail and what isn't. But you are still pretty sure everything is fine; you will come upon a milestone or a marker or a fellow hiker in no time and reorient yourself. You are probably just at the mid-way point of the trail so it is bound to look more pristine than the beginning section. Another 10, 15 or 40 minutes go by and you finally stop, spin around and realize that you can't even see clearly which direction you took to get here and that there is no clearly visible path and nobody else is in sight. You stand. You stand. You wait. You wait for some sign, some sound, some person, some connection or clue that might loop you back to the rest of the populated world.

Panic!

That ever happen to you? You should try it. I mean try not to get killed from exposure and dehydration while you are at it, but there is nothing like the experience of that rapidly descending panic. Churchill said there is nothing in life quite so thrilling as being shot at without actually getting shot! Indeed. Near encounters with disasters are rather precious. I had one of my earlier ones about two years into college. I spun around and realized I was somewhere I didn't want to be. I had come here. I had deliberately gotten here. Worked and fought and fretted to get here, but I no longer wanted to be here.

I made one last ditch effort to try and save my chosen course. I took a semester off from BU and went and worked as a phlebotomist at Mass General Hospital. A phlebotomist is the guy who comes to draw your blood. I would start my shift at 6am. Wander down the maze-like halls of that old and revered hospital. Visit various wards on different shifts. I figured I should actually spend some time in the environment that I might spend the rest of my working life in. How did this place feel? Is this where I belonged? Was this what I wanted?

The answer was a decisive 'No'.

All of a sudden I had no place to go, nothing to do, no direction to aim at.

As often happens, when we feel most lost and abandoned and foolish in life for the way we have been doing things and the dead-end we have arrived at as a result, something new opens up. And it did for me. The Muse called! I discovered photography. Within a few months, the hours I had previously been spending in Biology labs and Chemistry labs and the Programming rooms in the basements of BU got transferred to the long hours I was spending in the darkroom at UMASS Boston. I had a lovely, glum and stern teacher named Melissa Shook, under whose somber tutelage I started to believe for the first time that I might have the right to be an artist —

that my perspective, my take on things mattered. For the first time in my young life around the age of 20, I entertained the notion that my subjective experience might be as meaningful and valid as the scientist's study of the objective universe — that my feelings, emotions, perceptions and interpretations had a place in the physical world as much as the facts and figures about the physical world.

Photography has been a great love of my life. It has made me feel more at home in this world. It has made me see the continuity and the intricacy of this world. It has prompted me to love this world more. It has shown me that wonders are everywhere, close at hand. It has revealed that there is a hidden order in things waiting to be discovered if we look with enough patience and empathy, and that this order has seemingly unending layers. It has shown me that the experience of beauty is intrinsically woven into existence — at least into any and all existence that a human being is capable of experiencing through his faculties.

Photography even allowed me to not let go to waste my scientific proclivities. It showed me that an engineer's love for precision is very much applicable to the artist's endeavor as well. That art also demands study and theory and consistency and the understanding of the deeper theoretical relationships between its various elements. It has shown me that art also possesses its own theorems and hypotheses and it needs scientific study and testing and experimenting in order to grow and thrive.

## The Art & Engineering of Ecstasy

This combination of the Engineer and the Artist, the balance of scientific rigor with equal part emphasis on subjective perception is what I have brought to my study of Eros.

This unexpected journey into Eros began rather simply. I've been with the same woman for about 28 years now. We met in our sophomore year at BU. We've been together ever since. About a decade into our relationship, we thought it was time to start expanding our sensual repertoire a bit. Our dynamic in this realm has been—she sends me out to test the waters first, see what I find. If it's good, maybe she'll try it too. So I started reading more books about sex. I started taking classes in sensuality. I studied modern Tantra with teachers like Charles Muir, Laurie Handlers and Barbara Carrellas. I took classes going deeper into the erotic anatomy of women with Sheri Winston. I studied Pussy Stroking with OneTaste and later taught for them and ran their NY branch for over a year. I sought out the parent branches of OneTaste and studied with Morehouse in Lafayette, CA and The Welcomed Consensus up in northern California. And along the way, I discovered the dark and luscious arts of BDSM. I went to D/S retreats like Dark Odyssey and later taught workshops for them. In short, I studied. I pursued. A full tabulation of my journey in this realm would require a proper memoir. What I want to emphasize here is that I brought to my exploration of Eros the same nerdy drive for understanding, deciphering, cataloging, classifying and theorizing that I possessed as an incipient engineer/ scientist. And at some point in my journey, I realized that I had learned enough that it might make sense to start sharing and teaching others what I had learned.

So here we are. More or less. It's been a winding journey. This is not the sensible path the Indian boy had in mind for himself. Rebellion and recklessness are supposed to be the follies of youth. But I spent my youth on the straight and narrow. It's in my late thirties and now in my forties that life seems to have swung me into the outer fringes of respectability. How did I end up in a line of work that raises eyebrows?

## This Book:

I find myself having the same conversations over and over with students and coaching clients. Our problems are the same. Couples are stuck in the same bad patterns. Individuals are stuck in the same bad habits that keep sabotaging their joy and expression. The obstacles that people are facing in creating a rich erotic life are the same bunch of obstacles. Just as the foundational information around what causes a bridge to stand or to collapse does not change from bridge to bridge, the foundational information about what makes partnerships thrive or fail does not vary wildly from partnership to partnership. Human nature has structure. Human eros has structure. And the glitches and the weaknesses and the misperceptions that keep tripping us up are the same ones across the population.

This book is my attempt to articulate and organize these universal conversations regarding our emotional, relational and erotic lives.

## How To:

This is not a How-To book. I'm all for how-to exploration. My great desire is to give hands-on training to more and more people. I would very much like to live in a culture that understands the need for, and values, hands-on erotic training. I teach classes in Pussy Stroking. I teach classes in Rope Bondage and Spanking, Dominance & Submission and much more. Technique is important. Achieving a state of Mastery in one's Eros is not possible without real hands-on knowledge and skill, so I'm all in favor of training individuals and couples in the erotic arts. My next books may indeed be about techniques and methods. But this book isn't, because after observing and teaching people for many years, I have concluded that hands-on training is not where so many people get stumped. They get stumped BEFORE showing up for hands-on training! They get stumped in all the internal and interpersonal areas that don't even allow them to seek real education. This book explores those obstacles.

This exploration is the Prerequisite. The prerequisite to happier relating, to touching sublime states with a lover, to finding permission for ongoing erotic expression.

— — — — — — — — — — — — —

## Book Structure

This book has 15 chapters. They are divided into 5 sections — 3 chapters per section. Each section covers a different component of our Erotic Journey.

## The Chakra System

Eastern traditions believe our physical body is not the only level of our reality. We have subtle bodies underneath our physical body, and in these inner bodies there are energetic centers—chakras—that correspond to the various aspects of our psyche. Western psychology has a common model that divides our mind into the Conscious and Unconscious levels. The chakra system could be seen as a more nuanced, 7 tiered description of our Conscious and Unconscious aspects.

I find the chakra system a beautiful cheat sheet for the journey of the human soul. I refer to it throughout this book. You don't need to be a scholar of eastern mysticism to follow along. This is a very brief outline that will serve the purpose:

7th Center - Cosmic Consciousness
6th Center - Inspiration. Vision
5th Center - Self-Expression. Giving/Receiving

4th Center - Love

3rd Center - Esteem

2nd Center - Biological Sex

1st Center - Physical Survival.  Tribal Identity

— — — — — — — — — — — — — —

# MAN - WOMAN

# 1.  Dreaming of Wolves

(A chapter addressed to women)

'Where are the real men?'

I am hearing this lament from women quite a lot these days.  It's actually quite an incendiary statement.  I can only imagine what would happen if a man were to declare in a crowd of women, 'Where are the real women?'  Very likely something would be hurled towards his head in no time.  But that's a separate matter.  'Where are the real men?  What's happened to the men of today?'  It comes out more as a cry of frustration from women than any kind of real inquiry.  I think most of the women asking it are not even holding any hope that this question is answerable.  But let's explore it a bit.

What does the real man look like?  If he existed at one time but has now gone extinct, what did this species look like when it was still ambling the earth?  Ask women this and they are likely to give you examples in the form of movie stars.  This may seem frivolous at one level, but I think it is quite helpful.  We are reaching for archetypes when we do this.  And there is a wealth of information in archetypes.  Who are/were the real men?  Sean Connery.  Jack Nicholson.  Harrison Ford.  A generation earlier:

Robert Mitchum. Gregory Peck. John Wayne. Humphrey Bogart. Men's men. Men that nobody could ever mistake for a boy. That would have been impossible. Where have they gone? And what's wrong with these boy-men of today? How did we go from those men to these?

Want the short answer? It's this: You killed them off! By 'you' I mean you women.

'Impossible!' you protest. 'I've done no such thing. And besides, such real men were not so easily killed! That's what made them real men! That was one of their defining characteristics in fact. A woman could hurl anything at a real man and he would be able to take it. He is supposed to be unflappable. Everything from a woman's hottest passions to a woman's craziest tantrums, a real man knows how to handle it all, and to handle it all with a sly smirk and some mischief and a sense of playfulness. That's why we loved them so.'

Indeed. All that is also true. It is true of grown real men. It's true of men who have gotten the chance to mature into their realness and manliness. But right there is the conundrum—what if they are no longer given the opportunity to come into their fullness? What if you start finding them wrong for this realness and this manliness from early on in their life? What if you start steering them instead towards an entirely different ideal of manhood—one that is toothless and devoid of that strength, independence, mischief and competence that you loved in those real men?

What if the essential quality of the real man has always been a certain Wolfishness that resides in the male archetype? What happens when you declare open season on this Wolf?

Here's the state of women today: Imagine a lovely gal alone in her bed, writhing from her loins outwards, dreaming of the Wolf. 'Ohh, the Wolf! How beautiful you are! How powerful! How graceful! How ravenous you are! Come closer Wolf…. Let me run my fingers through your exquisite mane. Ahhh…come devour me you beautiful Wolf.' Then she opens her eyes. And perchance there is a real wolf somewhere in her sights. You know what she does? She screams bloody murder! 'Wolf! WOLF!!! Quick, get a gun. Shoot the wolf! Kill the wolf! Kill it!' The wolf is dead.

Pity the woman. Pity her aching loins. Pity the bleeding wolf.

Over the past 30 years you have all but killed the Wolf from the male psyche. Now you are lamenting his absence. Now you are crying in your drink, drumming your fingers and asking over and over, 'Where are the interesting men? Where are the men to make my pulse race? What has happened to them all?' Look behind you. Their heads are hanging on your wall.

## The Real Truth About Both Sexes

**A Woman:** A fully realized woman, a fully sexual woman, a fully turned-on woman, a woman full in her power — is a real pain in the ass! An empowered woman is not an easy woman. A fully turned-on woman who has claimed the range of her sexual desires and appetites is going to be more than a handful for the best of men in this world. A self-expressed woman is not a tame or a tamable creature. She will perplex you, overwhelm you, frustrate you, drive you nuts.

The sex of a fully expressed woman is so big and complex and ravenous that no one man can hope to keep up with it. She is bound to be too much for any one man.

**A Man:** A full realized man has a wolf in him. This wolf is ferocious and troublesome and untamable. The Wolf in the male archetype is inherently predatory. The Wolf has ready access to violence. The Wolf is driven by his appetites. And in the absence of cultural or legal interference, what prevails in the Wolf is a sterlingly primitive directive: Appetite is correct!

And his appetite has wide range and ambition. He is uninhibited and absolutely unapologetic about his desires and the length he is willing to go to satisfy them.

## A Brief History of The Sexes
**Men:**

I'm not sure when exactly this started, but probably at least 5000 years ago, the male archetype decided he wasn't going to put up with this fully expressed and impossible to control woman. So he started to dominate her non-consensually. He started to oppress her, to sabotage her sex by declaring it sinful. He created rules of propriety for the woman that all but castrated the woman. And if she refused to comply, he proceeded to literally castrate and kill her.

This domination and oppression continues till this day — much more prevalent and brutal in some parts of the globe than others. This male subjugation and sabotage of the female power has been the longest siege in our history.

In many parts of the world this siege against women is starting to wind down. It is not as bad as it used to be. But what that original, unobstructed woman might have been before the siege, we still don't know. We are getting closer to rediscovering her, and this is about the best we can do right now.

**Women:**
And how have women collectively adapted to being oppressed and subjugated and curtailed in their desires and expression?

We are all savages. We are very adaptable. Oppress a group in one way over here, and they are likely to find a way to gain advantage over there. Women have been denied direct access to power, so they have discovered and invented many indirect routes to power.

Women have become masterful at controlling the emotional lives of their men, and of their entire household.  They have become the silent puppet masters of their masters.  The men may continue to think they are the boss, and women let them think this while steering men's actions, emotions and resources.

This is a very abbreviated & stylized history of the war between the sexes, but for our purposes it will do.


## Modern Times

More recently, in the past 50 to 100 years, women have gained greater direct access to power.  And with that acquisition of power, women have declared open season on the Wolf who played such a direct part in the implementation of their oppression.

And women have truly succeeded in this battle.  You have succeeded not only in chasing the Wolf underground, you have gotten inside his head and made him doubt and hate himself.

Just as in centuries past women internalized male judgements and believed themselves to be dumber and more sinful and less worthy, many of today's men have pretty much accepted that anything masculine about them is in error.  Men today have started to accept that masculine traits are inherently stupid and backwards and paleolithic. Men have come to believe that they, in fact, are as simple minded and obtuse as women have been angrily accusing them of in recent decades.

Man bashing has become so pedestrian and widespread today that it doesn't even register on most people's ears. Men themselves have ceased objecting to it! It's just an accepted form of punchline across our culture.

So to women I can say, 'Congratulations! You have killed the Wolf!' Your success has now become your misery. This is why you are sitting through one insufferable date after another with a big fluffy sheep across from you who is putting your feet to sleep. This is why the desire to be really handled in bed and to feel ravaged and taken by somebody's skilled appetite is going unsatisfied encounter after encounter.

This is why you bought and read (and masturbated to) 100 million copies of a mediocre book—just to get an emotional hit of a gal being handled by a man who still has access to his Wolf.

This is why you are constantly torn between the practical need to hold onto the political, economic, and cultural gains you have made in recent decades, while at the same time you continue to dream of that infernal Wolf! Oh, the Wolf. Where are you? Why can't I have you as well as abolish wage inequities at the same time?

I actually think you can! That's why I wrote this book. Let's explore how.

## Breaking the Bad Loop

Women are craving love from men, with men. But they are running low on their approval of men. They don't see these two phenomena as being causally related. They think that because their experiences with men have been so disappointing, their feelings towards the masculine have logically and justifiably diminished. Their low opinion of men is merely derived from their life, from their experience. But the causality is reversible here.

If you are in a state of disapproval towards the masculine, you will never arrive at a state of adoration with men. You will never touch love. To reach for love where there is no approval is moot. It is a fool's errand. Can't be done.

If you want to act on this broken state, focus on approval first. See what you can do to repair your approval of the masculine. See what you need to do to regain (or have for the first time in your life) some modicum of RESPECT for the masculine.

Women don't think there is anything alarming or dire about this widespread lack of respect that they feel towards men. They think this lack of respect, once again, is quite logical and justified. Their own experiences have brought them to this state of disrespect for men. But take a step back from this and look at it. Here you are, clearly stating: 'I as a woman have lost all respect for men.' Then you follow that up with, 'I want to find true love. I want to find a man who adores me and wants to make me happy!' Do you see the absurdity? If you don't, try reversing the sexes in this scenario. Imagine a man who stands up and says, 'I have no respect for women. I think they are all crap. AND, I'm really looking for a great gal to make me happy, someone I can really care for and someone who cares for me.' Would you want to date this guy? Who wants to step up and take his hand and walk down the aisle? Or even sit across from him for a dinner date?

Men and women are in a dire, downward spiral. And most often, they are placing their bets on the wrong probability. Women keep saying, 'But that's why I'm looking for that great guy! The ONE! I am looking for the guy who is going to restore my faith in men! I'm looking for a guy I can *finally* respect!' I would only point out your dismal success rate in this search. It hasn't panned out for most of you.

So my recommendation for success is that you don't wait for the perfect guy to show up before you confront and dissolve your abysmal rating of the male psyche! Find a way to arrive at approval of men first. Find a way to dissolve your anger and disappointment first. Find a way to arrive at some respect and adoration of the masculine first.

Most women I suggest this to push back so immediately and reflexively that it often feels to me that their disapproval of men is some kind of a treasure that I am trying to wrench away from them. If holding onto that disapproval of the masculine is such a strong desire in you, EXAMINE THAT FIRST! That is your real trap. There is no getting past that. There are no happy stories that can be created IN SPITE of that.

# FADD: Feminine Approval Deficit Disorder

Most men on the planet are suffering from this ailment right now. It's a pandemic. Men have oppressed, violated and humiliated women for a few thousand years. Women have struck back by withholding what men deeply desire and crave and need from women — women's approval.

Women's response to millennia of nasty patriarchy is understandable and justified. But where do you want to go from here? Do you just want to continue punishing men for what all men have done to all women for thousands of years? Fine if you do. It's your prerogative. But then please quit any desire for romance or love with men. You can't have both.

And if you want to move towards love and romance and softness and adoration and great sex with men, then you are going to have to put down your sword of disapproval. It's a mighty sword indeed. And collectively, this mighty sword of women disapproving of men has created an entire generation of broken and confused men.

Men are often likened to dogs and women to cats. Let's use this handy metaphor here for men—wolves & dogs! There are a variety of ways (a spectrum actually) of how

FADD impacts the masculine. And that impact can be compared to what happens to dogs when they are mistreated.

At the cowering and timid end, if you beat a dog too much or disapprove of him and bully him, he will simply not have any self-esteem. He will be scared and groveling. He will always have his tail between his legs and that frightened, hounded expression in his eyes. — — THAT is the hen-pecked man. He is constantly apologizing. He is constantly trying to placate the woman. He is too weak to make the woman feel assured or protected in any way. The woman feels that, if anything needs to be done, she better handle it herself. Such a man is afraid to handle his woman sexually. At best, he might be able to follow some direct instructions. At the core of such hounded men is a ball of rage towards women. Because even in the heart of that beaten down mutt, there is a wolf howling somewhere, and he hates what he has become.

In the middle of the range we have men who are almost as scared as the hound-dog, hen-pecked man. But the men in this range have developed a whole set of defensive mechanisms and personae to hide their fear and insecurity. They are busy covering up their fear of women with bravado and trash talk. They too are terrified and unsure of handling a woman sexually. They generally rely on routines and repertoire in sex. They probably prefer pornography to real women. Most of your dates come from this wide spectrum of men.

The men in this wide middle-band are becoming increasingly deceitful and slimy. Their word isn't worth much usually. They know how to present enough of an attractive persona to seduce women, but their surface game hides a very deep anxiety about their inherent worthiness— their worthiness in this world and their worthiness to their women. These men have very little capacity for going deeper in their relationships with women. They have very few emotional tools to rely on when relationships take a challenging turn. They jump ship fast when challenges show up. Often times, they jump ship preemptively anticipating that things are going to go bad.

The dangerous end of the FADD spectrum is the junkyard dog. The beatings and disapproval that these guys have received have made them aggressive and hostile towards women. At their core they are as afraid and resentful of the feminine as the cowering hound-dog or the middle spectrum of guys that range from the nice-guy to the pick-up artist. But the men at this end of the spectrum are even more defensive about the uncertainty they feel towards women. These men have pretty much given up trying to win with women. They have turned predatory and sociopathic. Their stand towards women is war-like: I'll do whatever works to get from women what I want from them.

So yes, the field report on men out there is quite dismal. But what I would love for you to try and see, the shift in point of view I wish you to have, is that all these men have been MADE this way by a steady diet of FADD for most of their lives!

The Dogs out there are defective. And you women have been abominable dog owners!

Now, what do you want to do about it? How do you want to break the cycle?

(And I'm not saying here the men themselves don't have a boatload of work to do at their end. They very much do. But this chapter is for you gals.)

## Forgiveness → Approval → Love → Ecstasy → Soul

The difficult but obvious answer is: You have to start with yourself first. If you keep waiting for the population of men to turn healthy and balanced and brilliant on their own while the women continue to bombard them with negativity and disapproval—that's just not going to happen. If you think you will somehow beat the odds and stumble upon one good dog in the vast pack—that's not entirely impossible, but then the unfriendly question I would have to ask you is this: Why would such a good dog pick you as their owner? Why would such a good man want to be with you if you are still entrenched in your disapproval and disrespect towards the masculine?

Start with yourself. That's where your personal and soul journey is also. Doesn't even matter if you end up finding the great guy that turns out to be the love of your life. If women as a whole started bleeding out of their system all the venom that they are holding towards men, this world would become a sunnier place.

It is inarguable that men have done a lot of crappy things to women over the past few thousand years. But that is exactly why we are in desperate need of a massive forgiveness ritual for women towards men! There will be no real progress without that, only a continuation of a self-fulfilling prophecy. Your stance that men are meager and disappointing will keep generating men who are so and you will keep dating such men, one after the other. The passage of time will only provide you with more and more evidence to calcify your disappointment and anger towards men. And you will die a bitter, bitter woman. Your choice.

And it goes without saying that if you do release your misgivings and your resentment toward the masculine, that is not going to magically transform the men around you instantaneously. You will continue to come across men, on the street, at the work place, on your dates, who will continue to fall short of being that happy, proud, loving and well-balanced dog, who also has access to his mischievous Wolf. But it would still be a better life. It's a step in the right direction in a big way. It's much better to have a solid and sane dog owner working with a dog who is still a bit off, than to have a miserable and abusive dog owner with a dog who is already nutty from a lifetime of mistreatment.

The Masculine is in deep trouble these days. But one thing the male population and the masculine archetype has not lost from its core is its fundamental adoration of the female. We adore you! We live for you! We know it in our heart and in our bones that our life would be meaningless without you. So have faith in that! When that deep need and desire to be close to the feminine is nurtured in some real way, sanity and balance start to burst through all the layers of nonsense and defensiveness in men. This is the only long game between men and women that has any real potential for bringing a new paradigm of relating into our world.

— — — — — — — — — — — — — —

# 2. Men Are Terrified of Sexual Education

We live with this myth that men want sex more than women do. Men are kinkier than women. Men are more desirous of trying newer and stranger varieties of sensual and sexual play, while women are more inclined to seek romance and security and occasional, respectful and temperate sex in one of 3 officially approved positions. Men are brimming with uncontrollable urges, wanting to chase everything in heels, and women are poor wallflowers searching for softness and connection while bravely trying to protect the hymen from the brutes!

It is true that even today, even in our most sexually liberated areas of the world, women are less inclined to voice their desires as openly as men do. The reason for this has a great deal more to do with PERMISSION. Men have always enjoyed greater permission for voicing and pursuing their desires. This discrepancy might create the impression that men want sex more than women. But it's simply not true.

My knowledge in this area is anecdotal, not scientific. I have not gone out and done an exhaustive survey to determine what I am about to state here. I'm only going by my own experience and observation of people in my workshops, coaching sessions and communities:

- ◆ Women have a GREATER appetite for sex than men.
- ◆ Women's desires and fantasies regarding kink, domination/submission, consensual non-consent, pain, sadism, masochism, and humiliation are bigger than men's.
- ◆ Women feel more than men.
- ◆ Women feel more pleasure than men!
- ◆ Women's desires and appetites span over a wider range than men's.
- ◆ Women are sexual omnivores.

Women are sex!

And men are lost!

Women are the ones brimming with urges and desires and fantasies that will make your local teamster blush and close his manly thighs. Among the couples I encounter, pretty much without exception, it's the women who are dying for more play, more adventure, more handling, more kink, more experiences, more variety, more freedom.

And their men are sitting next to them looking stiff and terrified like they've just been called into the principal's office.

The men today are overwhelmed. The men today are under-skilled. The men today are faking their sexual mastery as much as women have been faking their sexual pleasure for eons. Most men have no idea about what's stirring inside their women, and most of them have no idea how to access all that is stirring there and play with it.

## Obstacles

There are two big boulders sitting in the path of today's men:
1. The education you are getting is quite off the mark.
2. You are afraid to seek real education.

This chapter is mostly about the second boulder, but let me cover the first one briefly. The education most men are getting is through porn. I'm not going to present a long, well-argued case on why getting your sex education through porn is a bad idea. I'm just going to state here that getting your sex education from porn is a bad idea.

I'm not any kind of a teetotaler when it comes to porn. I actually think that, in a truly sexually liberated culture, there has to be a space for enjoying erotica in many a sundry form—film, writing, live performances, erotic open mic nights. Eros should find a welcome entry into any and all areas of our lives—cuisine, fashion, art, poetry, fiction, theater, choreography. I'm all for us enjoying erotic services for money as well. All of these can enrich our lives when done with some awareness and panache.

Porn or visual erotica turns problematic in these 2 ways:
1. If it is your primary outlet for sexual expression, interaction and release, over an extended period of time, your ability to interact and sex with a real human being will diminish.
2. If you think what you see in porn is what real sex is supposed to look like, your real sex life will become problematic.

Let's address the second obstacle mentioned above: Men are afraid to seek real sex education.

Why?

Ego!  And fear of sexual self-evaluation.

Men are very defensive when it comes to admitting that they are not as skilled as they would like to believe they are.  They are afraid to show their ignorance.  They are afraid to show their level of doubt in this area.

An even greater fear that keeps men from seeking real knowledge is this:  Once they get the real knowledge, they will realize just what mediocre lovers they have been so far.  This is a very big hit to the male ego.  It's like finally getting a real report card of yourself as a lover for the first time.  And this report card is not just your grade with your current lover.  It is your grade for ALL the lovers you've ever had.  Imagine that!  That would make for a hard day.  To come home with a little note in your hand with a big C - on it for the lover you've been your whole life.

Men are so terrified of getting this hit that most of them would prefer to continue believing whatever they have been believing about their sexual prowess, even if there has been faint evidence to support their beliefs.

Predictably, the older the man, the longer the track record he has as a lover, the greater the fear of getting this bad report card.

## Hopeful Sex

Much of the time, the men who come into my classes act like self-proclaimed experts — Casanovas one and all. In truth, most men are having sex with their fingers crossed behind their back. Most of them are doing little more than relying on routines they THINK have worked in the past. "She seemed to have made a lot of noise when I did this last time, let me try it again and hope she likes it again." Or, "The LAST girl I was with seemed to make a lot of noise when I did his, let me try that on this one and hope she likes it."

There is a lot of HOPING going on in men's sexing right now.

Or they are trying to reproduce something they have seen in porn. They might have grasped on to some visual and act-oriented notion of what good and hot sex is supposed to be, and they are running through their check-list of acts and activities to fulfill that contrived criteria, once again hoping that if they do it like the professionals in the videos, they are doing well.

Most men are utterly lacking in the skill to feel their woman in the moment. That's because most men are not in touch with their own body and its inner feeling. Most men are in their head or entirely checked out during sex. Or at most, they are in touch with their isolated pleasure and simply using their partner to scratch their own itch.

## The Tenderest Spot

I really do appreciate how crushing it can be for a man to hear that what he's been doing with his woman isn't working for her. I know this emotional terrain well because often it is only after this conversation has happened between a couple that they seek out some education or counseling to try to improve things.

Just the prospect of sitting with their woman in front of a third party — be it a therapist or a sensuality coach — and have their woman express that she is dissatisfied with her sex life is deeply humiliating for men. One can perceive how tender men are in this area. Just looking at the men in such moments, it's easy to see how desperate they are to please their woman sexually and make her happy. So the denial or avoidance that comes out of this tenderness is understandable. But the only way forward is through honesty and real learning.

My invitation to men is this: It's possible to KNOW with certainty what is happening in your sexing— with yourself and with your woman. It is very possible to take the guesswork and Hoping out of your sexing. Seek real knowledge. Replace your doubt with real information. Replace your defensiveness with real Mastery.

[And do it in a hurry! Because it feels like the dissatisfaction and piss-off level that the women out there are feeling at not being handled with skill is reaching some kind of an epic scale in our society—and with good justification. Their men are not delivering in sex. And women deserve better! The male ego needs to make way here for real progress to occur.]

## From Hope to Mastery

The cornerstone of sexual mastery is being present in your body and feeling what is happening right here/right now instead of being in your head with your formulas and notions.

If you acquire this crucial skill of feeling your own system and your partner's system in real time, there is one question that you will stop asking your woman: 'Was it good for you?' You won't have to! If you are so out of touch with her feeling body that you can't perceive her sensual ride in the moment, then it's irrelevant what you are doing, what acts you are engaging in. The real art is in being able to feel each other's inner terrain. The real art is in being present and live with the sensations that you are creating in each other's bodies NOW. Move from routines to attention.

You are going to have to let go of what you think you know. You are going to have to let go of techniques that you think can be a stand-in for real attention. And once you learn the art of attention, please come to class and learn some REAL technique. Come learn how to really touch and stroke pussy! Become masterful at engaging the clitoris and the pleasure zones inside the pussy. Come acquire real skill in the darker arts of Dominance & Submission play. Learn rope bondage. Learn how to safely and effectively do impact play like spanking and flogging and so much more. Come seek real information and training. Start a journey in the erotic arts.

And, god help you, you are going to have to erase a lot of porn files from your cerebral hard drive and forget that you ever thought you were seeing depictions of good sex and how it's supposed to be done.

Seeking mastery in the sexual realm is your birthright. I know you want to excel here. I know you've already sought information, read about it, and tried things in an effort to acquire mastery. If the information you had been absorbing and assimilating had been good, you would indeed be masterful by now. But alas, we are living in the sexual dark ages. Even with half the World Wide Web laden with porn and sex, you'd have to get in there like Diogenes with a lamp in your hand to look for the few honest nuggets. The misinformation is massive! You've been misled.

Here is a cheat sheet of 3 important skills to get you started on your path to real sexual Mastery:

## 1. Your Attention Is Your Greatest Asset As a Lover.

Put all your other techniques on the shelf for now. Pay attention to your attention itself. Are you present? Are you here now? Put your attention on your woman now. Feel her now. Observe her now.

Our attention is what brings information about the world back to us. Whatever you put your attention on, it will start to reveal itself to you. What information is coming back at you about your woman when you put your attention on her this moment?

Tune into this listening. Double check the information that is coming to you to make sure it is the real thing and not your own mind noise. Confirm your listening and keep honing it.

Never get so lost in activity or technique that you lose all sense of your own attention. If need be, pause your action so you can come back into just your attention. Pause to look. Pause to listen. Pause to take in. Let your attention go out towards your woman, and let that attention bring back real information in real time about your woman.

## 2. You Need to Feel Your Woman.
So Feel Your Own System First!

The key to feeling your woman is feeling yourself. The information about the other's system is available, and it is available inside your own body! This may seem ironic or convoluted at first, but it becomes very plain when we examine how is it that we feel ANY emotion in others. We feel the other's emotions because their emotions resonate in our own body, and technically we feel only our own body. The process is very simple and mechanical in a way.

You can use one of our other physical senses as an analogy: The sounds that our brain perceives are not directly connected to the sound waves that are around us. Our brain only perceives and interprets the functioning of our ORGAN of hearing. Our brain communicates with our ears only. How the various components of our ears move and vibrate and resonate determines the sound we hear. If our instrument of hearing is off or impaired, if our ears become damaged or occluded, then our brain will perceive distorted or incomplete sound as a result.

With our emotions (and turn-on), the same process is taking place. We have an INSTRUMENT OF EMOTION. It is a bit less visible than our ears and eyes. This instrument resides inside our body. When you feel an emotion, try tracking the emotion to your body. You will find it there. You will find a heavy or sweet weight in your chest or a giddiness in your head or a lump in your throat or a fear and churning in your rectum or a queasiness in your stomach or swirls of turn-on and arousal in your groin. This is our inner body, our emotion body. It is our emotional organ singing and sounding in various ways.

When two people are intimately engaged, their emotional organs begin to resonate with each other like tuning forks. If you are in touch with your own tuning fork, it will give you information about your lover's tuning fork!

Being tuned in with your lover in this fashion is the path to real mastery. You need to feel your woman. You need to feel her system. And the only way you can do this is if you are present with your own emotional body.

**Being in such intimate connection with a lover can be confrontational!** Each person's capacity to stay present during high sensation is limited. This is one of the main reasons that people check out in sex in the first place! It's easier to be in your head with your routines and memory or even fantasy. It takes a certain inner 'caliber' to stay present when there is a lot going on in our feeling body. Staying present during high sensation is equivalent to holding on to a live wire. It is challenging. Since the masculine mind is more naturally inclined towards mechanics, men tend to 'exit' out of presence into action and routines when holding onto that live wire becomes uncomfortable.

Your woman is always going to be too complex to be satisfied with any technique or routine. No method is going to work exactly the same way twice — not even with the same woman, let alone from one woman to another.

Unless you are really feeling your woman, you will keep walking on eggshells of doubt and uncertainty as a lover.

## 3. Transparently, Be Who You Really Are.
This third point may not sound much like sex advice, but it is a much needed overarching character asset that today's man is in dire need of. Boldly and cleanly be who you really are. Don't fake it. Don't finagle. Don't polish yourself into something else. Whatever your assets and shortcomings, be upfront and unapologetic about them. Neither try to hustle others into thinking you are more than you are, nor apologize for not being what others

wish you were. Put an 'As Is' sign on yourself. Take it or leave it!

To reach this state of transparency, you are going to need to deal with all the places you currently find yourself inadequate and are busy covering up. You are going to have to deal with your areas of shame and discomfort that you have cleverly buried under the rug hoping nobody would notice. Granted, this type of housecleaning can often be a long arc in itself, but my encouragement here is that you get started. When men deceive and lie, turn hypocritical, nothing good comes from it—for ourselves, for our place in the world, for our relationships— to women or to other men. So I urge you to clean house. Stop hiding and pretending. If there are changes you want to make, take action towards making them. For the rest, accept who you are and show it to the world without hesitation.

This level of integrity is essential if you want to touch Ecstasy with your lover. Pretending and faking is not going to work. Being a good guy is not going to work. Putting in a lot of effort is not going to work. You, genuinely being who you are, is an essential aspect of the journey towards Ecstasy.

If you somehow manage to finagle your way to Ecstasy while wearing your false masks, you may just end up creating a spiritual crisis for yourself! Higher states of consciousness have a way of blasting our nonsensical identities. So, too much of your mask may get ripped off very quickly if you manage to carry it that high.

The more advisable route is that you start peeling off your masks yourself before reaching for Ecstasy.

— — — — — — — — — — — — —

# 3. Men Win. Men Lose.

Women are missing out on men.
Women are not making the most of their men.
Women don't know how to get the best out of their men.

Women today are like a comedic character who does not know how to drive a stick shift, but who is driving that stick shift anyway, in spurts and starts, taking 15 minutes to drive 2 blocks before giving up in a huff, kicking the tire while smoke pours out from under the hood.

Women really need to learn how men function. It will make everyone's life easier. The trouble is this: just as the car itself can't give you lessons in how to drive a stick shift, most men can't help their women understand men. You need mentorship. You need a little practice behind the wheel with an instructor sitting next to you. That's what we are doing here—helping you get the most out of your stick shift car/man.

## Men Want to Win.
The winning men want is something women know very little about. 'Win' is the best word to describe the

phenomenon at hand, but how women may conventionally understand winning (and by contrast, losing) is not exactly what internal winning and losing represents in men.

Conventionally, winning and losing are paired in a zero-sum equation. Someone wins / someone loses. But the winning and losing that men experience is not this kind of zero-sum set up.

Men are not interested in winning OVER women. Men desperately want to win WITH their women.

If his woman is winning with him (is happy with what he is bringing to her life), the man also wins. If his woman is unhappy with what he is doing/acting/creating/bringing/offering to her, the man loses.

Another distinction: nobody is DECIDING this win! The man is not sitting there judging and determining, 'If my woman acts this way towards me, I'll consider that a win; if she acts another way, I will consider it a loss.'

His winning and losing happens rapidly and without his interference or influence. His winning and losing happens in RESPONSE to the response of his woman.

This winning and losing simply happens at a phenomenal level in the hearts and souls of men. And it is very straightforward, and it is impossible to manipulate or rig. In its straightforwardness, you could say that it is downright mechanical:

Man offers X to woman. Woman likes man for offering X. Man wins because woman is happy with what he gave her.

Man offers X to woman. Woman dislikes man for offering X. Man loses with woman because woman is unhappy with what he offered her.

Imagine there are two little lights stuck in the chests of men: green and red. When he feels he has won, the green light goes on. When he feels he has lost, the red light goes on. HE HAS NO CONTROL OVER THESE LIGHTS HIMSELF! He is not deciding when one or the other goes on. He is not judging you when he loses. Nor can he help loving you when he wins.

Really…just treat this system of his as if it were robotic. It is not personal. It's just the way we are built from our core. Green light. Red light. A Win. A Loss. The gal that can make that green light flash and flash again will remain in our heart. We will cross deserts and mountains for you. Why? For our own selfish reasons—because that green light blazing on in our chest is what we live for. And if you are a woman who can make that light come alive, we will seek you and find you and cherish you.

Conversely…every time that red light flashes, men die a little. We get smaller. We feel smaller. It hurts. The more we lose with a woman, the more we want to escape from her company. We feel we are not doing any good being around her anyway. She doesn't seem happy with us.

If you as a woman cause that red light to flash, take some responsibility for it. If you say 'Well, that's just your stupid light; you deal with it', you are being disingenuous. Men are no more solitary creatures than are women. Men are excruciatingly susceptible to women. And I don't think this is much news to women! You make regular use of this susceptibility of men towards you, so also take responsibility when what you do and say makes him feel he is losing with you. You are a participant in this. In fact, you are almost entirely at cause. I will say it again, we men ourselves don't have any direct control over this green or red. Because, believe me, if we did have control, not unlike some lab rats on cocaine, we would just sit on the couch blinking away our own green light and giving ourselves that feeling that we are winning. It would be better than masturbation.

This also does not mean that men's win-loss configuration does not change and evolve over time. It does. Part of a man's maturing is very much tied to his grappling with the challenge of loss and failure in life. The more a man evolves, the more he grows into his character and finds his place in life, the less potent and less frequent that red light gets. But on any given day, at any given hour, a man is not in control of what experiences in life register as a win or a loss. So if you really want to learn to operate men, accept their green and red as a given. Whatever makes him feel he has won with you will bring you closer together. Whatever makes him feel he has lost with you will drive him away.

## Men WANT to be Well Used!

In fact, one of the most effective ways to pull your man out of his doldrums is to use him well.

How to use a man well:

1. Give him a task he can succeed at.
2. When he succeeds at that task, let him see and feel how his action and accomplishment made your life better.

Men have a singular relationship directive: MAKE WOMAN HAPPY!

If they succeed in making Woman happy, Man win! If Woman unhappy, Man lose.

## An Unhappy Woman Is A Losing Proposition!
This may sound harsh, but it is gospel!

There is a common saying often heard down south, 'If Mama ain't happy, ain't nobody happy!'

Show me a miserable household and I'll show you a miserable woman at the center of it. At the heart of every miserable marriage, you will find a miserable wife. No man has left a happy woman!

NO MAN HAS EVER LEFT A HAPPY WOMAN!

No man has ever left a woman he was succeeding at making happy. Our woman's happiness is our bread and air. Your happiness is our paycheck. That's how we want to be paid in our relationship for our efforts. If the woman is unhappy, we are pretty much starving and pay-less. And a woman we can't make happy is flat-out a losing proposition.

Look at men when they are emerging from a break-up. You will find them in this broken, pay-less state of failure. That red light in their chest has been flashing and flashing. They've been getting smaller and smaller in their relationship. They have been drinking and sighing for a while wondering how much more of this they can take, or should take, or how much of this is USEFUL to take. There is no point in being with a woman you can't make happy.

When men stray and have affairs, the driving motive is once again those two lights in their chest. Women would like to believe that men are dogs and they are always chasing a younger piece of ass or a prettier piece of ass. The fundamental truth is this: they are chasing any woman who can make that green light in their chest come on. They are chasing women they feel they can win with. They are chasing women they feel they can make happy. They are seeking that emotional bread and air that they so desperately need in their relation to women—approving women, women who know how to use them well, women who are happier because of the contribution the man is making to her life.


## The Myth of the DEMANDING Woman

Women often make the mistake that men are lazy and they want the easy way out, that they prefer easy women compared to a complex woman with complex needs.

Men actually prefer demanding women! But you have to really understand what this means from a man's perspective:

For a man, succeeding at satisfying a woman with big and complex needs is a BIGGER win! We don't mind the challenge, as long as the challenge is an HONEST one. And the challenge is honest if, when the man delivers on what is being demanded of him, the well-deserved REWARD is waiting for him. What is that well-deserved reward? It's the same—a happy woman. If we know that bringing you a single flower is going to make you a little bit happy, but bringing you a bouquet is going to make you more happy, each man, every single time, is going to go for the bouquet! The equation is simple for us—we want the biggest win we can get our hands on.  But if a bouquet and a single flower generate the same level of happiness in you, then we may not think it worth the effort to gather 20 flowers when 1 will have the same impact.

However, how women generally understand the notion of being a 'demanding' woman is something entirely different.  Most women think being demanding means 'not being easily satisfied'.  Or worse, NEVER being satisfied.  From the male perspective, such a woman is not a possibility for a bigger win; she is a proposition for perpetual losing!  'No matter what you do, no matter how hard you try, you will never succeed at making me happy.'  Most marriages end on this note!

A woman who insists on being unhappy, unsatisfied, dissatisfied in life is pretty much guaranteeing her ongoing failure with men.  From a man's perspective, she is a bad investment.  She is like a boss who will never pay you no matter how hard you work for her, no matter how much you produce for her.

## Learn This Win-Lose Mechanism Of Men!

The modern, liberated woman tends to be quite vocal about how men are not showing up fully, of the skills and techniques men ought to learn and master in order to be better candidates for dating and sex. And I'm all for that! It's great that women are getting more demanding. And I personally feel men have been lagging in stepping up and acquiring the skills they need in order to deliver better in their relationship and their sexing with women. But this here is one skill that women desperately need to acquire. Learn the Win-Lose mechanism in men. Start paying attention. Observe your man. Tune into his heart. Become sensitive to these green and red lights on his chest. If you become interested and start paying attention, his inner experience of winning and losing will become almost as apparent as if there were actual green and red lights on his chest.

And this skill is not just for your romantic relationships. You will learn an incredible amount about ALL men if you tune into how they are experiencing their wins and losses in life, how every little thing that women do and say to men can make the red or green come on. Men are terribly tender in this mechanism. I will say one more time: We don't govern this mechanism. It governs us. We are at its effect. And we live by its guidance. We are built to chase that which gives us a win and to avoid that which gives us a loss.

Start paying attention to this in all the men around you and you will acquire some empathy for the hearts and souls of men. Extend this to your relationship with your brothers and fathers and sons and other men in your life.

Once you tune into this phenomenon, once you are able to see it plain as day, the CHOICE of the matter will become very apparent to you. What kind of woman do you want to be? One who is constantly leaving men smaller after she is done with them? Or one who leaves her men bigger?

## Maneuvering a Man by His Green (Cheat Sheet)

Learning to guide and maneuver a man by his green and making winning requests is an art form that woman direly need to learn. For women who have been entrenched in their disapproval of the masculine, this transition takes deliberate practice over a stretch of time. Here is a cheat sheet for how to influence your man, offer him guidance and give him productive feedback without creating a loss for him:

Hate the sin. Love the sinner!

Approve of the man first. Then give him information on how he might do things differently that would make you even happier and cause you to approve of him even more.

And before you get out your laundry list of all the man-improvement upgrades you would like to program in his system, take a 6 month sabbatical from your agenda. Simply start appreciating and acknowledging him for everything he is doing right ALREADY! This is a hefty spiritual practice for a woman. It will reveal to you just how much your ego is addicted to handing out disapproval.

More bad news: You are going to have to entirely give up the tone/energy/activity of whining and complaining. That is all red-light energy.

## PLEASE Start Driving on the Green Side of the Road

Here's how I know that women actually are already intuitively familiar with the green and red lights on men's chest: They've been trying to operate men by the wrong light!

Women are deeply trapped right now in their disapproval of men. This is as profoundly a spiritual matter as it is a relational one. There is a lot of forgiveness and housecleaning that needs to happen between women and men for us to truly move forward into a new paradigm. Give Green a try. Women everywhere today are very busy failing with men. Women seem hellbent on making sure men keep losing with them. The disapproving of men and masculinity has become our cultural modus operandi. Handing men losses, treating them like morons and punchlines, speaking as if it's a foregone conclusion that men are base and gross and lazy and stupid and useless — all of it has become normalized.

But how is this stance working out for you gals? How is poking the chest of your men till that red light keeps on flashing and flashing working out for your romantic and intimate relationships?

Give Green a chance. Give approval a chance.

And if just the idea of APPROVING of men raises your hackles, please do some spiritual work and clean out your system and bleed the man-bashing out of your soul.

Until you are able to enter into winning relationships with men, until you learn the art of driving your man by his green light rather than nagging him with the red one, there is no hope of any great loving or friendliness or sensuality in your exploration.

You will never get the best out of your man if he his losing. You will never get the most out of your man by trying to drive him with your disapproval and your dissatisfaction. Cannot be done. Has never been done. Will never work.

Shedding your disapproval of men is part of your journey as a woman.

Shedding your addiction to your misery is part of your spiritual journey.

Creating a winning relationship with your man needs to be an aspect of your genius in this world and a part of your self-expression as a woman.

Dare I say, restoring some RESPECT for men and the masculine in your heart is a deep and true aspect of your spiritual journey as a woman.

The possibility of entering into Ecstasy with your man depends on it.

[Actually, the survival of the planet may very well depend on it. At the heart of the man-woman crisis is the anger and disapproval women are harboring towards men.]

## If you become a green woman, you will be SO FAR ahead of the curve!

Most men have never met a woman they could consistently win with! If a man meets a woman he feels he can win with 50% of the time, he feels the gods have smiled upon his fortune. If you can learn the true art of creating a winning relationship with a man, you will become a rare creature who will be prized and pursued by the male archetype.

Men are tired of being driven by women who have no idea how they actually operate. With their unskilled and counterproductive handling, we don't get to drive as fast as we are capable. We don't get to bring our best and show our best in relationships. And our gears are worn and bent from all the losing.

Learn this fundamental aspect of the masculine, and you and your man will be zooming past everyone else down the relationship highway.

Also, don't try to look for any role models for this kind of winning relationship in the media, in movies, in novels, on TV. It does not exist in drama and literature! Why? Because drama is driven by conflict and dysfunction — two characters whose interests are pitted against each other in a zero-sum struggle to the death. The winning relationship I am describing is built on a foundation of friendship. It is built on two people genuinely interested in making sure that both parties are winning and having fun and getting off. When such a relationship is present, there is no drama in it! It does not lend itself to narrative. It's too peaceful. It is too celebratory.

And one of the peaks of that together-celebration is Ecstasy.

— — — — — — — — — — — — —

# FRIENDLY RELATING

# 4. You + 1

What's possible between you and a lover?

How far will you two go?  How high?

Will you soar together?  Look at each other in wonder afterwards, in awe at the journey you just took?  Or will it be a low flying affair?  Dragging your shoes in the dirt the whole time, awkwardly dancing out of step and off the beat?

We've all had our share of the latter.  And I'm sure there are those peak experiences in our memory — moments we have shared with a lover during which we felt transported and uplifted.  Those are moments we might describe with words like Ecstasy, Joy, Bliss, Union.

Is there a more reliable way to create more of those transcendent experiences and leave behind the dragging-in-the-dirt dates and make-outs?  Are there any factors to consider?  Do we have any control or choice in this matter?  Or is it incidental 'chemistry' between strangers in the night?

I believe our peak experiences are not random or accidental. There is structure behind why we are able to touch those high notes together with a lover.

To gain clarity on the matter, it's helpful to pull back to a wide-angle perspective and examine just how many different ways there are in which we show up in our relating to ANY & ALL the people in our lives. If we can understand the spectrum of all of our relating, it will become easier to understand the nature of our Ecstatic relating.

## Why +1?

Q. Why relate to anyone at all? Why can't we do without relating altogether?
A. Because we need others.

As human beings, we have many needs. A few of these needs we may be able to fulfill on our own, but most of our needs require us to be in relation to another.

Let's acknowledge that, at the ground level, we all are selfish and self-interested. If we could attend to all our needs without bothering with other human beings, we would. It would probably be more economical, safer and less troublesome. But that's not really an option we've been granted. We have needs that cannot be fulfilled by us alone. We need others to fulfill our needs. We need others for our selfishness.

Can we quantify and qualify our various needs, so that we may examine how each kind of need prompts us toward a specific kind of relationship with another human being?

## Hierarchy of Needs - Eastern Style

Let's examine our needs through the chakra model. For this conversation, we can just divide that system into 'Higher' and 'Lower' centers. The first 3 centers constitute the lower; the rest fall in the higher.

My premise in this whole conversation is this: There are two basic forms of relating: Higher and Lower. The lower forms of relationships are economical—a means to an end. The higher forms of relationships are intrinsically valuable. In the higher relationship, the relating itself IS the point. Being in those higher forms intrinsically improves our quality of life and our joy.

Let's examine the lower centers to see why relationships that are hatched here tend to not have much of a chance at moving our soul or touching Ecstasy:

## The 1ˢᵗ Chakra Marriage

The 1ˢᵗ center is about Physical survival — Material needs. Food. Earth. Dwelling. Shelter. Physical existence and safety.

The relationship that is solely based around the needs of the 1ˢᵗ center will be about necessities and survival. This is a very pragmatic exchange based on a sensible evaluation of how being with a particular partner increases our chances for physical survival and promises to improve the quality of our physical existence.

Marrying for money and security falls in this category of 1ˢᵗ Chakra Marriage. Most marriages have traditionally fallen into this category. Marriage as an institution has been about property. It has been about the bride's parents making sure their child is going to be taken care of, that she will have a good and safe household, that she will have physical comfort.

Even from the perspective of the husband, a good 1$^{st}$ Chakra Marriage would imply the woman is strong and in good health and will be a resource to the household, to the running of the house/farm/shop/business. The husband perceives that his physical existence will be easier and better and happier with this woman/partner in his life.

A 1st Chakra relationship does not need to be a marriage. An employer/employee relationship is primarily a 1$^{st}$ center contract.

The giving-receiving balance for a 1$^{st}$ center relationship is very important. The only reason to have this kind of bond is if both parties feel that by making the bond, they are both going to come out ahead. A successful 1$^{st}$ center bond is a win-win material deal for both parties. It is a happy commercial exchange.

What also lives in the 1$^{st}$ center is Tribal Identity. Wanting to marry somebody from your own tribe is also a 1$^{st}$ Chakra impetus.

There is an enormous amount that can be said about the functioning of the 1$^{st}$ center and the space it occupies in our lives and in our culture and society, but in this conversation, we are narrowly focused on the various reasons/needs that prompt us to get into relationships with one another.


## 2nd Chakra Marriage

$2^{nd}$ center is about sex. Biological sex. Procreation. Basic Sex. NOT Ecstatic sex which is the point of this whole book. Nature's sex. Getting the job done: organ in organ, fertilization, gestation, voila! —brand new body coming into the world, slimy and loud.

The sex that goes no higher than the $2^{nd}$ center is truly more nature's provenance than our own. Nature reigns here. We hardly need to be present for nature to do her job. Sex will happen. And procreation will happen.

In the workings of this center, Nature most profoundly displays her genius.

We may make a lot of fuss over our mating rituals. We have a lot of tradition built around the officiating of mating partners in all of our cultures. But the bulk of what is happening here is Nature's Sex! Our big brain merely provides the awning and the wedding feast and the fancy rituals. All of it is extraneous to the priority and agenda of the 2nd Chakra. Birds do it. Bees do it. We send embossed invitations and drop fortunes on weddings to do it, but the genius of this center is really in our biology itself.

To truly appreciate the genius of the 2nd center, it's actually better to turn our attention to the animal kingdom and leave human mating rituals aside. Examine this area with the fascination and curiosity of a scientist to appreciate nature's genius in inventing the sexes and creating behavioral and biological mechanism by which to create new life and new bodies. Nothing is more complex. Nothing is more awe-inspiring than sex when you see what sex is down to its very depths.

It's everything from a bird song to the double helix!

If God tips his hand anywhere in existence, it's in all that sex is. I mean creating the cosmos was pretty neat. Creating life was another masterpiece. But in creating sex, he really took the game to a whole other level.

## The 3rd Chakra Marriage

3rd center is our Esteem center! Big topic! A very HUMAN center. All animals do the 1st and 2nd centers, but when we reach the 3rd we are acquiring our humanness.

The concerns of the 3rd Chakra constitute the majority of the noise in your head if you live in a relatively safe and secure and functioning regime and have your basic needs met. When our stomachs are full, our esteem is our preoccupation.

We need others desperately to grapple with our esteem. We cannot arrive at it alone or measure it alone or make any sense of it in isolation.

The 3rd Chakra marriage is a marriage that raises our stock by association. We want to align with those who raise our value. All bonds formed with this agenda are 3rd center marriages of one sort or another.

## 3 Means To 3 Ends

These first 3 centers are economical or transactional in nature. They are concerned with me me me first. All the relations that we create from these 3 centers are relations in which we treat the other as a MEANS TO OUR END. We are users in these centers. We use other people for our needs. Our own needs are always more important to us than the person we are attached to from these centers. The relationship is rational and useful as long as it is serving our needs.

This is not to say that these 3 centers and their needs are base or deplorable. They are what they are. They are unavoidable. They are very human. They certainly are our starting point in the relationship journey.

Even within this economical relating, our attitude and approach towards our partner can vary over a broad spectrum. At the friendlier end of the spectrum, we are straightforward and business-like in our relations at these 3 centers. We speak our needs openly. We try to strike an even bargain with another so that we may both get what we want.

At the darker end of relating in these 3 centers, we are hustlers and liars and seducers and manipulators. We are capable of being consummate conmen, downright grifters, in all the ways we can twist and hustle each other to get our own needs met, while screwing our partner. We are constantly finagling to come out ahead in the bargain — to be the winner rather than the sucker in the transaction.

These 3 centers, and the things we do to fulfill the needs that live here, often don't make us look particularly noble. So be it! You can try skipping out on these 3 levels of relating by becoming a celibate and a renunciate. That is one possible path. It's not my favorite one. There is a lot of rich terrain here in the lower realm. Better to go into it and experience it fully. Eventually you will come out the other end.

These lower realms hold the components of our humanity that keep us alive and functioning. Without them, our physical survival would become precarious. Indeed, those people who are particularly weak or ineffective in the functioning of these 3 basic centers tend to have a touch-and-go relationship with physical life.

## Higher

What about the centers above the lower 3? What are their needs? What do the relationships that we form from those centers look like?

For this conversation, it's more productive to just draw out a broad comparison between the Lower Relating and Higher Relating:

- In the Lower Relating, we are interested in others for what they can do for us.
- In the Higher Relating, our interest in the other is intrinsic. We are INTERESTED in them. We are fascinated by them. We are drawn to them.

- In the Lower Relating, we are constantly on the lookout for a good deal where we might end up having more than the person we are relating with.
- In the Higher Relating, we start to feel a wonderful sense of happiness and purpose when we are able to GIVE to the person we are drawn to. Being Received by the other is a kind of bliss. We want to give ourselves away.

- In the Lower Relating we are always trying to control others so that their changed configuration might serve us better.
- In the Higher Relating we are very much interested in the self-expression of our partner. We are curious to see what they are becoming. We want to contribute to their self-expression. It is fun to do so! It's an adventure to see our partner find the new within himself or herself. We share in and contribute to their discovery and journey.

These Lower & Higher levels of relating are something that all of us are doing all the time. We all have economical and business relations. We often categorize them as being 'not personal'. And then we have our personal relationships with lovers, friends, family where the people are intrinsically valuable to us. And as is the case in all matters human, the lines are often fluid and blurry.

Even within a relationship, we are capable of sliding between levels. New relations may start off as incidental or economical and grow into friendships and intimacies. And the opposite is also common. When intimate relationships start to deteriorate, often all that is left between the couple by the end are the bare pragmatic reasons for being together and not parting ways yet. Quite often, by the time a couple seeks help or therapy for their troubles, they have been relating with each other primarily from the lower 3 centers for quite some time.

## Replaceable You

This higher level of relating need not mean you look upon your lover as a deity. But if you are not able to look upon him/her with some genuine affection, fascination, adoration and curiosity, if you don't feel a true desire within yourself to contribute to the expansion and journey of your partner, then your relationship may be functional and convenient at best.

Such a relationship will also be easily replaceable. If you are not enamored with the unique soul of your partner, if they are merely serving a need in your life, then it will not be terribly difficult for you to find another person you can use for that same need.

If you keep this last point in perspective, then perhaps it isn't particularly tragic or even surprising that the vast majority of romantic relationships fail quickly after they begin. They begin in the lower 3 centers, where the bonds are fast and loose. A replacement molecule is waiting around the corner.

## Ecstatic Relating

Let's recap the 3 Means:
Treating another human being as a means only works at the lower 3 centers.

1.  You can use someone else for your material survival and security.

2.   You can use someone for your sexual release and gratification.

3.   You can use someone to prop up your esteem.

Ecstasy is not possible from these levels.

Examine the motives for any of your relationships.  If none of the above 3 motives is present and you still feel a pull towards this person, then something interesting might be possible!

To say that a relationship is INTIMATE is to say that your motives for that relationship are above the 3rd center.  And the motives that live above the 3rd center belong in the category of life that we loosely refer to as SPIRITUAL.

Intimate relationships that are not spiritual are meant to deteriorate!

If your partner is a means to an end, you are on the wrong level of relating to be able to touch Ecstasy.  It would be like throwing your head back in order to see the stars while you are standing inside a building.

Get to the roof first!

The stars don't live right at the roof, but from the roof you can leap skyward.

— — — — — — — — — — — — —

# 5. Thou Shalt Communicate Clearly, Powerfully, Lovingly.

Sending someone a dead fish wrapped up in newspaper and a bulletproof vest is a communiqué. Dead fish, severed heads, stone cold looks, withdrawn absence or silence. A handful of dishes hurled across the living room, a lobbed brick. A courtly bow, a raised fist. From a haiku to a manifesto. The range of how we can and do communicate is so vast as to pretty much blanket all human actions and creations. Every gesture and tone, that smirk, that nod, that exhale, that sigh. All of it is communication.

One would think that with such a vast array of communication channels available to us, humans must be masters of communication, masters of mutual understanding and empathy.

It can be so. 2 people can become masters of communication and empathy towards each other. Only 2 small conditions are needed:
1. You have to be genuinely interested in understanding your partner.

2. You have to be a stand for your partner's ongoing self-expression.

Clear, powerful and loving communication between 2 people is a conspiratorial undertaking. Only as long as I feel that your interests and my interests are the same, that your self-expression and mine are tied together, will our communication stay clean. If we are on the same side of the line, there is a shot at building this communication and empathy that supports both of our lives and future.

If you are on the opposite side of the fence from me, if we are in an adversarial relationship, if your winning would mean my losing, then the dead fish or the hurled brick might in fact be a better communiqué, a more effective one.

It isn't bad or hurtful communication that is the source of frustration and ill feeling between couples. It is their stance towards each other that is the source of it all. If you are in a zero-sum game with your partner, you don't stand a chance. If you think your partner getting what he or she wants will mean you *not* having what you want, then you are buggered. Loving communication won't help; it won't occur really. We don't communicate lovingly with enemies; we communicate to undermine them, deceive them, convince them, outwit them, confuse them, weaken them, beat them.

## Talking to the Enemy

Most couples live in enmity. They live in a zero-sum psychological equation with each other. That soil does not bear vines of loving communication. That is the soil of battleground. Guile is needed there. Exploiting the other's weakness is needed there. And we are all great warriors. We shine in these zero-sum games really. We are deceitful and wily and predatory and manipulative. We know how to weaponize even our weakness and tears and helplessness. We are full of ingenuity in the struggle for getting our way. Getting it from another, over another.

And our entire battery of communication modalities serves us in this battle.

So move your focus from communication to stance. If you are in a bad space with each other, your communication is prone to be tainted. If there is piss-off and resentment, your communication will carry shards of your piss-off and resentment. These shards will create

91

further hurt. They will further erode your friendliness and create a downward spiral. Know this. Know that if you are angry with your partner, if you are disappointed, your communication is going to be dirty.

The only good communication that can happen at this stage is communication that is genuinely attempting to repair the anger and disappointment and piss-off. You should be communicating in an attempt to return to friendliness towards each other. That's the only real task at hand.

Needless to say, in most relationships this does not happen most of the time. Resentments fester for long periods. Anger is left un-diffused. It gets under the skin and under the words on an ongoing basis. The whole relationship sours under the weight of this unresolved unfriendliness. Eventually a couple arrives at a stage where all communication from one's partner feels loaded and hostile. Everything has a destructive undertone. All that the couple can hear from each other after a while is the subtext of hostility.

When this has occurred, it would be incorrect to say that the couple is communicating any more. All their communications have become salvos. The words, the silences, the looks are all pregnant with disapproval and pain.

And this is usually the state in which a couple shows up seeking help! At one level this is understandable. This kind of ongoing hostility, where every word exchanged carries hurt, is a hell to live through. It's like living in a war zone. It is very stressful. This level of misery and hostility tends to create an ultimatum for a couple: 'Alright, we really need to find a way to do something about this, or let's just part ways! We can't keep going like this.' And so they show up on the couch of their therapist or counselor or life coach or pastor or whoever.

The body language at this stage tends to be pretty consistent. Put the couple on a two-person sofa and you will see each of them sliding to opposite ends. Each will grip his or her end of the sofa like they are hanging on for life. That 10"-18" gap between their thighs might as well be covered in burning coals. That no-man's-land gap between bodies always speaks volumes.

It's a painful and heartbreaking sight. These are two people who selected each other! These are two people who at one point felt they had found that special someone they wanted to share their life with. These are two people who saw qualities in each other they admired and wanted to import into their own lives.

Now, their bodies are poised to avoid contact. The danger in that gap between their bodies feels palpable from across the room.

How did they get here? Have they changed so radically since their first meeting? Have their values entirely shifted from then till now?

There are many paths you can take to arrive at this state of misery. This book is all about such treacherous paths, but in this chapter I want to focus on the one big path to hell that belongs under the banner of 'Communication'.

## The Sin Of Expectations

Expectation is a sneaky mechanism. You have to examine it a little to understand how pernicious it is. Because on the surface, having expectations of our partner feels like a healthy and normal thing to do. Of course we have expectations! Why shouldn't we?

The problem does not lie in any single expectation you might have. The problem is in the MECHANISM of expectations. The mechanism of expectations tends to function as nothing short of a fission reaction in relationships.

Here's how the mechanism of Expectation goes:
You hold an expectation.
Your expectation is met.
All is well and good.
You hold another expectation.
Sooner or later, that expectation will not be met.
This unmet expectation creates feelings of anger and resentment towards our partner.

*Now comes a little poison pill straight from the devil's pharmacy:*

Your expectation mechanism now generates ANOTHER EXPECTATION that your partner will recognize, acknowledge, make amends for the anger and resentment they have generated in your system by not meeting your initial expectation.
Want to guess what happens next?
They don't!
Your partner probably was not aware of your initial expectation, or they forgot, or slipped up or whatever. They don't feel responsible for your upset. And they

don't acknowledge your follow up expectation that they make amends. Which leads to:

Further resentment + expectation that your partner will address your 2nd generation upset and resentment.

Which they don't.

Which leads to…which leads to…which leads to.

Expectations generate a progeny of piss-off. A tall stack of misery. A closed loop of feeling angry, dismissed, disrespected, neglected, unappreciated. Till we are in no-man's land — with clenched teeth and a gap of burning coals between bodies.

This accumulation of unfriendliness is a big destroyer of relationships. It's likely the biggest destroyer of relationships. To keep living in this state of festering resentment is a pretty miserable way to be, and probably not a very physically healthy way to live.

If you have arrived at this unfriendly stance with your partner, the only priority should be to get out of the unfriendly stance and back to kinship. The only communication you should be doing is the kind that is attempting to restore friendliness.

# You Can Be Right or You Can Be Happy

Most people chose the former. We choose it many times. It takes a bit of living to realize that the payoff of being right over being happy actually isn't all that great.

The real un-wisdom in this stance is not realizing that succeeding at being right OVER your lover is also a losing stance. Even if you won the argument, by making your partner feel bad and small and apologetic for not meeting your expectations, you have only further eroded your relationship, not enhanced or fortified it.

The goal of communication in a relationship, especially when the couple is in an upset, should be to repair a relationship towards friendliness. And the most important step you can take towards this goal is to pinpoint the poison pill of unmet expectations in your relationship. Make a list of all expectations that are repeatedly not being met, and take some radical steps to eliminate them from your relationship by any means necessary.

Unmet expectations are the cancer of relationships. Find them early. Cut them out.

Most couples don't do this. Unfortunately, even much of the help or counseling that they may receive at this stage might not encourage them to quite do this. Most couples end up communicating their DISPLEASURE at the unmet expectations. And then they do it again next week and twice again the week after. They think they are exercising their self-expression by this communication of displeasure and anger and resentment regarding their unmet expectations. Not so! You are in fact giving succor to the cancer.

Think of the end stages of your last relationship. You should be able to spot the tumor of unmet expectations. You are probably still bitching about it, still self-expressing your disappointment, your outrage at the unmet expectations, still boring your drinking buddies with examples of how bad, how unreasonable your last partner was about meeting your expectations of them.

By the time you are in the land of 'self-expression of my unmet expectations', you are deep into the zero-sum stance. Your partner has long stopped being that comrade-soul whose self-expression was your pleasure and happiness. That partner has now moved on to the other side of the line. Their non-compliance, their lack of caring is now the source of your misery. You are losing because they are doing or not doing something. And if you are to ever be happy again, you must continue to try to make them act differently. Any communication that grows out of this adversarial stance is likely to increase the distance, increase the hostility between the two of you.

## From Expectations to Agreements

An expectation is a relationship contract that you prepared, but one that your partner never signed!

If there were a court of relationships, all expectations would be thrown out by the relationship judge when you file your complaint.

YOU HAVE NO RIGHT TO HAVE YOUR EXPECTATIONS MET!

Why?

Again, because your partner has not agreed to meet your expectations.

If your partner agrees to meet a certain expectation, then you have created an AGREEMENT. Agreements are valid contracts in the relationship court.  Expectations on the other hand are just surefire structures for creating incrementally nasty breakdowns in your relationship. And once this breakdown is underway, all your communication will turn hostile.

*If your relationship is not built on a solid set of agreements, your communication is already sabotaged!*

Make clear agreements.  Keep your word.  Good communication will follow.

Excise EXPECTATIONS from your psyche and your relationships and replace them with AGREEMENTS!

Agreements that are being upheld and honored are the true foundation of any thriving partnership.  Whereas expectations have a tendency of creating implosions, explosions and collapse, agreements have the power to fortify the structure of your relationship and even offer quick repair when things do go haywire.

If your relationship is built upon solid agreements, your communication will practically sort itself out and become friendlier.

Agreements need to be clear. They need to be expressly defined.

Agreements should be written down!

Agreements need to be agreed on! If your agreements are authentic, then by their very structure, they will be / should be a win-win scenario for the two of you. Your agreements should put you both on the same side of the line.

Your agreements should support and preserve your stand towards each other.

Agreements should be re-visited on a regular basis. They need to be changed as the need arises so that they continue to serve both of you. Agreements need to be 'living documents'. Sometimes I think many a marriage might have taken a different route if the couple had pulled out their wedding vows every Sunday night and checked-in for an hour on how they were doing with them.

Our desire for a deep soul connection is genuine. Those inspired wedding vows are written with the best of intentions. But intentions are not enough. Relationships are about stamina. Being able to touch Ecstasy requires stamina! If getting there were easy or obvious, we wouldn't need a path. But our journey is a long arc. And Ecstasy is a high milestone on this arc. To reach it together, two people need that ongoing friendliness towards each other. Can you imagine touching Ecstasy with someone you are full of resentment towards? It's an absurd proposition! We need the chops to deal with the challenges that a life together is bound to hurl at us without turning into enemies. If two people have that clarity and that bond, then it's very possible to touch great heights together. It's, in fact, inevitable.

— — — — — — — — — — — — —

# 6. How Expensive Is It to Do Business With You?

How do you react when things don't go your way? When you hear something that jostles you? Or bruises your ego? How easy are you to bring news to? Bad news. Awkward news. News that is not going to tickle your insides and make you feel grand.

How expensive do you make it for people to speak the truth?

How expensive do you make it for people to speak their mind, especially regarding you? To say to your face what they think of you? If your lover starts to tell you what isn't working with the way you are showing up in the relationship, the way you do the things you do, how do you respond? Where do you go internally? How do you make your lover feel for communicating with you honestly?

If I took a survey of your friends and lovers and family and asked them these questions, what is the consensus that would emerge? How have you made them pay for doing business with you?

What's your general response and modus operandi when hit with unpopular speech regarding yourself?

Do you defend? Do you go right on the offensive? Make the other person wrong? Are you immediately propelled to even out the scale by picking on the other person by pointing out all their shortcomings?

Throw a fit? Cry? Curl up in yourself and weep and become pathetic and wounded?

Throw dishes? Raise your voice? Withdraw in silent contempt and pain?

Become physically imposing or threatening?

How expensive do you make it? How do you make them pay?

Guilt trip? Start collapsing and go into breakdown? Avoid and disappear?

Pretend not to hear? Create a diversion?

Attack back with charm? Distract and confuse?

Or are you vindictive?

Do you go for a cerebral attack? Get all intellectual and analytical and tie the other person in a knot?

How do you avoid the pain of hearing that someone is finding you lacking in something? That they do not think highly of you in some aspect? That someone is unhappy enough with who you are that they may want to retreat and break relation from you? What's the sleight-of-hand you pull for avoiding the pain of being found lacking, of being not desired, of being rejected?

Whatever your reactionary/retaliatory modus operandi is for avoiding this pain, think of it as being your particular flavor of a treacherous foundation for the construction of a relationship with you. Pick your metaphor here: If you throw angry fits and go on the attack, your foundation is volcanic, can't build on that. If you avoid and divert and shift blame, your foundation is like wet mud; can't build on that. If you practice emotional blackmail and sink into breakdown and cry, your foundation is like quicksand; can't build on that. If you avoid and run, your foundation is a steep hill; can't build on that. If you practice obfuscation and confusion, your foundation is watery; can't build on that.

Most relationships collapse in one or another of these states. The lack of communication, due to the high price of communication, finally reaches a breaking point.

Often, towards the end of a relationship, one or both people finally dump on each other all their withheld piss-off, all the things they feel they have not been able to say. All that heavy, delayed communication lands on whatever un-solid ground that has been present throughout the relationship. The building collapses. Exit disaster area. Try again elsewhere. Good luck to you.

Those few who are able to move past such a relationship crisis and build something new together, without exception, are able to do so because through some method or mediation they start to take away the cost for their partner communicating what he or she needs to communicate. They create a solid and even ground for all the withheld communications to land on. If you can sort through the mess of unsaid things, clear it all up, then, just maybe, you have a shot at entering a new phase in your relating.

This aspect of our nature — the cost we extract from others when they express themselves around us — is a cornerstone for our relationships. People put all kinds of nonsense in their romantic profiles. Most of that stuff doesn't amount to anything. I don't need to know how good-looking your are, how many degrees or hobbies you have, how big your dick is or how ample your tits are, how good you are at going down on your lover or what a mean frittata you can conjure on Saturday mornings. None of that matters long term. And none of that matters when you've hit a road block or a plateau in your relationship.

On the other hand, tell me on a scale of 1 to 10 how expensive you make it for people to speak truth to you, and I will put money down on how long any of your relationships are going to last. That's solid information! You should get that measurement from your date before going out.

## Stifled Relational Expression = Stifled Self Expression

Having a rich and thriving sexual life is nothing other than each partner finding his or her ongoing self-expression in eros. Self-expression is key. It's the business we are in. Where self-expression is ongoing, you are in flow, you are in good business, you are in good partnership. If you are holding a field in which your partner's self-expression is encouraged and supported and called forward, you are an amazing lover and partner. Conversely, if you are holding a field in which your partner's self-expression is stifled or threatened or punished, you are a crappy partner and you are stifling your partner's soul journey. There really isn't that much wiggle room here.

It may take people 3 weeks or 15 years to burn out of that stifling relationship, but the process is the same. The stories have a million variations in their specifics, but the underlying theme is consistent: Where your self-expression is ongoing, you will want to continue. Where your self-expression has stopped or is being blocked, you begin to die.

So what field have you been holding for your partners? You think people find greater self-expression around you? Do they feel free to express themselves? Free to speak what they are thinking and feeling? About you? About themselves? About their desires? About what they want next in their Eros?

Or is your field restrictive and worrisome and oppressive? Egg shells and land mines all around you? Everyone better tread lightly!

## Pain Management

What is at the core of this expense we tend to extract from others when they speak the difficult truth? What is really at the core of those fights, that defensiveness, those obfuscations and denials and deflections in all our relationships?

Pain!

It's the pain we feel when we are found to be NOT ENOUGH. This pain is one of the deepest cuts!

We all are inclined to push back against this pain. Our individual styles differ. The goal is the same. Whether you retaliate, deny, avoid, deflect, distract, attack or run, whatever color rabbit you pull out of your hat here, the rabbit's purpose is one and the same—to not have to confront this pain head-on.

This pain of self-doubt regarding our inherent worthiness is our most tender spot. It's a core 3rd Chakra issue. Wherever in our constitution this doubt is more prevalent, we are likely to be expensive to do business with.

When our doubts are triggered, when our SELF-doubts are triggered, we are going to snarl and bite back. We are going to want to hurt or avoid or justify.

## To Self-Loathe Is Human

To want to avoid pain is understandable. Trouble is this: we are all rife with pain triggers! Pangs of self-doubt are ineluctable in the human experience. We are all walking masses of wounds and triggers. We all have shortcomings, real and imagined. We are all trying to put our best foot forward. We are all hoping our good qualities will carry us over our bad ones. We are all hoping our lovable qualities will outweigh our less admirable aspects.

This hope and denial mechanism is very human, but in the longer run, over the long arc of our soul, it is our crucible. These pain triggers are the stuff that needs tending. This is where our work and attention need to go. And the longer we delay taking on our doubts, our self-loathing, the more trouble it creates in our relationships.

Your pain and your bracing against the triggering of your pain will make it expensive for other people to do business with you.

Your pain and your attempts to avoid this pain are the number one destroyer of love and intimacy in your life.

Your pain and your attempts to not feel it will preclude the deep and authentic relationships that your soul is craving.

Your pain and your wounding stand like boulders and ravines on your path towards Ecstasy.

Your pain will make it difficult for others to speak the truth to you, to criticize you. It will be harder for them to express their desires in front of you. It will be harder for them to tell you what they really think of you.

## Tell Me How to Lie to You

What can you take? What can you hear? The people in your life are actually taking their cue in these matters from you! We are all taking cues from each other regarding what we should and should not broach with each other.

Nobody wants to be the bad guy. If people perceive that a certain communication is going to take you into breakdown, they are going to avoid being the bad guy/gal who pushes you into breakdown! And if they perceive that their difficult communication is most likely to boomerang back and slap them in the face (because of the way you take such news), then they are going to find a more subtle way of dealing with you. Or avoid it entirely. They will look for a side door to exit out of being in a relationship with you. They are going to lie to you. They will lie to you because they perceive telling you the truth is going to be too costly for them. And they are right! You've made it costly!

## Expensive People

- People who have not dealt with their own emotional triggers.

- People who often respond with petulant reactionary behavior.

- People who live in the belief/reality, 'If I'm feeling it, it must be true.'

- People who believe, 'If I'm feeling bad, you must have done something bad to me.'

- People who regularly go on about how someone else 'MADE THEM FEEL'.

- People who believe there is an overlord class of people (or a whole gender) that is making their lives miserable and disempowering them.

The core piece here is: Lack of Personal Responsibility / Victimhood Identity.

If you are harboring a victimhood identity, you are pretty much pain waiting to happen to the people in your life. You are a grievance looking for a cause. And OTHER people are always the cause.

## Victims Are the Most Dangerous People in the World

Pretty much every heinous ideology in the history of humanity has been constructed on the backbone of the Victimhood Identity. Pull up the speeches of the Third Reich and you will hear victimhood! You will hear the argument how the proud German people have been marginalized and humiliated by the powers that be and all that they are trying to accomplish is to nobly restore themselves and their people to a state of pride and decency. Listen to white supremacists in America or Europe even today and you will hear the same narrative of victimhood identity.

Victimhood is a flytrap for the human ego: Victims are always right! Our ego lives to be right! Moreover, Victims are always JUSTIFIED in whatever they do to their perpetrators. That is some big license to possess!

Be suspicious of any person anywhere wielding the victimhood card. 'Bad things have happened to me' is not an indefinite license for retaliation or vindictive behavior. To live on this planet is to encounter moments when we are treated unjustly. If I'm walking down the street and somebody hits me over the head and steals my wallet, I am absolutely a victim and that person the perpetrator. But this Victim/Perpetrator marriage should be as short lived as possible. Hold the perpetrator accountable under the law and be done with the transaction. If you can't find the perpetrator, practice forgiveness and release, then be done with the transaction.

## GET OUT OF THE VICTIM/PERPETRATOR CONTRACT AS SOON AS POSSIBLE!

A victimhood identity, on the other hand, is built on the opposite philosophy. The victimhood identity is a long and faithful marriage between Victim & Perpetrator. It is not a happy marriage; it is not a loving marriage. Often times the marriage is a bit lunatic because the Perpetrator has long vanished, but the Victim stays loyal to the marriage. Often times, the Perpetrator never even quite existed, but the Victim still remains steadfast to the ghost spouse—because the alimony of the victimhood license is too sweet to give up for the human ego.

Untangling our victimhood identity is a crucial aspect of our soul journey! To fail here is to add misery and distortion to our own life and to the lives of the people we encounter.

## The Allure of Victimhood

Why is this dissolution of victimhood easier said then done?

The victimhood IDENTITY is like heroin for our ego!

To be RIGHT!?

To be right OVER other human beings!?

To be JUSTIFIED in our retaliatory and vindictive actions and behavior towards other human beings!?

There isn't a better proposition or stance for the human ego than this in all of creation! The privileges of the Victimhood Identity are pretty much custom-designed for the Human Ego.

Think of the perfect sniper's perch—some place high, with a wide open view, some place with lots of great, impregnable cover. That perfect perch is what Victimhood Identity is for the blood thirsty sniper of the human ego. From the cover of victimhood, we are able to strike with impunity.

## Loving the Snipers

As far as personal relationships with people who are harboring strong Victimhood Identities, it's akin to giving a warm hug to a land mine. People who are entrenched in their Victimhood Identity in fact have no room for a Beloved in their life! Their victimhood is their genuine Beloved! Their victimhood is their one true lover! This energetic geography is not very different from what a junkie looks like in the throes of his/her addiction. The drug is the Beloved. The next hit is the one true yearning. The chemical high is the one true love. There isn't any room for an actual human being to enter and form a connection.

Victims are the most expensive people to do business with.

From a spiritual perspective, the Victimhood Identity is the equivalent of a ditch on the human path. If you fall into this ditch, pretty much the only next step available to you is to find your way out of this ditch first—to shed your Victimhood Identity. No forward motion is possible until then. To have genuine intimacy with a Beloved will be impossible till then. And certainly, no path to Ecstasy will be open to you until then.

The only company you will succeed in keeping while in this ditch is with others who are in the Victimhood ditch with you! This is what makes the Victimhood Identity so potent and pernicious. Throughout the course of human history, entire populations have fallen into this ditch together and thereby given themselves license to be right over others and thus act in heinous and destructive ways towards 'the others'.

Any narrative of Us versus the Others should be a red flag. Chances are that this narrative is being hatched from inside the Victimhood ditch.

## Ask and You Shall Receive

If you are unsure about how expensive it really is to do business with you, if you are unsure about how often you tend to fall into the Victimhood ditch and blame the people in your life for your emotions, ask them! Ask them nicely and they will tell you. Make a resolution to create a more open permission field around you, and people will tell you the truth about you. And if at first this request that people in your life tell you the truth about how they have been editing themselves around you creates a stunned and worried silence in your friends and lovers, chances are you have been very expensive to do business with so far.

## Feel the Pain Without Reacting to the Pain

Reactions to pain are an attempt to ward off the pain. All the pain you ward off will either go and create an ulcer in your stomach or in the stomach of the people around you.

The key here is not to deny the pain or to be stoic or indifferent to pain or to even transcend it. The requirement of the human trek is much more brutish. Feel the pain and keep feeling it till the pain is all felt out and done with you! This is how we actually dismantle the triggers that are stuck in our system — let them excruciatingly ring and ring till there is no ringing left in them.

Stop making other people pay for your pain — even when you feel that other people are the cause of that pain. This may sound like a tall order. It is. This is also why so much of humanity and human relationships are in the shit so often. This is the test for being a grown up on this human ride. This is the prerequisite for your evolution on the human path. This is the prerequisite for creating a field in which love and intimacy and ecstasy may become possible.

## Truth In Sex

If self-doubt and insecurity are the core reasons why truth-telling becomes so expensive between people, then it's easy to see why truth-telling is always extra difficult in the erotic realm. No other area of our life is more fraught with insecurities. In no other area are people protecting themselves as well as their partner's ego more than in their sex life.

Lying to protect your partner's feelings is as real a problem as making it expensive for people to speak truth to you. In the sexual realm, women are especially burdened with this flavor of care-taking lying. Women have been carrying their men's egos for millennia now. On the surface this may seem like a kind and loving thing to do, but it has powerful repercussions. Here are just 2 big ones:

- Anyone you feel you have to constantly protect from the truth, you will not be able to respect. So the more you carry your man's ego, the less you will think of him. The more you feel that he can't handle the truth that you are withholding from him, the less of a man you will feel he is.

- The more you protect his ego, the more you will put yourself in a care-taking role. The more that either partner goes into the care-taking archetype, the more Eros dies. Care-taking and Fucking are incompatible.

Breakthroughs in our Eros come about when we are able to make discoveries and express ourselves freely. The whole journey hinges on the revelation of new and TRUE information about the desires of the two people. If there is no permission for expression, Eros will be stifled. Ecstasy will be precluded.

— — — — — — — — — — — — — —

# DESIRE

# 7. Desire's Architecture

'Desire is like a bridge.'

I speak these words in my coaching sessions often. Most of the time it comes up while I'm counseling long term couples on how to regain some of the heat and passion and raw sex they used to have access to in the early part of their relationship.

What is a bridge? When is it needed? What function does it perform?

There are 2 criteria involved with bridges and desire:
1. A gap.
2. A desire to close that gap.

Desire IS the desire to close the gap—between yourself and another.

## Desire Problems

According to this model, when things are not going well in the desire department, things have gone off the tracks in one of two ways:

1.  There is no longer a gap to bridge.
2.  You no longer have a desire to bridge this particular gap between yourself and the other person in question.

These two problems are structurally and emotionally quite different.  And the remedies for them need to be different.


## The See-Saw of Desiring and Having

In order to have a thriving relationship over the long haul, a balance is needed between Desiring and Having, between experiencing a gap that one longs to bridge, and experiencing the joy and fulfillment of bridging that gap — by being with one's lover, enjoying them, relishing them.  Too much of one or the other creates problems and distortions in the Desire equation.


### Too Much Desiring

If you have set your sights on a shore that is very desirable to you, but it's a shore that you will never be able to bridge, you have set yourself up for a life of craving and deprivation.  Falling in love with an 'unattainable' person creates this kind of craving ride. You can set your sights on a person who is married, or lives far away, or someone who has expressly communicated they can't be with you. By setting your sights on the unattainable, you very effectively create this gap of desire that cannot be bridged.

You will even find instances where people say they are in love with someone who is not of a matching sexual orientation. This is setting oneself up for a life of pining and longing and dissatisfaction. This is a life of drowning one's sorrow in sad songs and glasses of white wine or bourbon. This ride can seem to have a lot of feeling in it. But often times, these feelings are a sham.

Setting your sights on a shore you can never reach is often a way of not engaging in life at all. It's a ploy for avoiding entering into a relationship. You remain on the side lines; you risk nothing; nothing happens in your life; time keeps passing by.

Pining for a lost love or an ex-lover or even a dead lover can take the form of this life of craving— all Desiring, with no possibility of Having.

**Too Much Having**
The more common imbalance that many long-term couples face is the imbalance of too much Having. You

found someone you liked, someone you were drawn to. You found an attractive shore you wanted to bridge the distance to. And you did! You started a relationship; you grew that relationship. You may have moved in together or gotten married. Now, the desire has become elusive.

Desire is a Bridge.

Visualize this: There are two shores facing each other, with a gap between them. The two shores want to connect; they want to touch each other. So they invent the brilliant device of a bridge. Wonderful! Satisfaction, Romance, Touch, Sex, & Enjoyment ensue.

Now imagine that the shores start inching towards each other. The shores move closer and closer together. The gap between them steadily diminishes. They keep getting closer till the two shores are touching. The gap is gone.

Is there a need for a Bridge now?

Basic Design Principle: FORM FITS FUNCTION.

The *function* of the bridge has disappeared with the meeting of the shores. If the function of bridging the gap is no longer needed, the *form* of the bridge/desire will correspondingly disappear.

## The 4 Arts of Desire

To keep desire alive, 4 different arts are needed. These arts correspond to 4 different aspects needed to create an active and thriving dynamic between Desiring & Having.

1. The Art of Wooing and Seduction.
2. The Art of Having and Enjoying.
3. The Art of Creating Distance.
4. The Art of Remaining an Attractive Shore.

## 1. The Art of Wooing & Seduction

Of the 4, this art has received the most attention throughout our history and our culture. I think it has received too much attention. Wooing and Seduction, especially as they are narrowly defined and practiced most commonly, are overrated!

The typical scenario of what this phase looks like can be taken right out of *Romeo and Juliet*. Boy sees girl. Boy is taken with the girl's comeliness. Boy wants girl. Boy woos girl—writes poems, shows up under her balcony, serenades her and so forth. The goal of this wooing and seduction is to get to the FIRST kiss, to the FIRST sexing, the first episode of HAVING.

I personally don't put much stock in the first kiss or the first moments of intimacy between lovers. The first time may be good or bad or mediocre. What does it matter? I want to see what two people are able to create together over the long haul.

The first Wooing & Seduction is pre-touch. It is more anchored in Craving than Having. Often times, this variety of Wooing & Seduction falls into confusion when the lover who is being wooed actually says yes! There are plenty of people who seem to enjoy this Wooing & Seduction of a new partner more than anything else. To them, even having the lover say yes, even successfully seducing them and finally having them is anti-climactic! The chase is it for them. This overemphasis on the chase of the new lover indicates that the person doing the chasing is more hooked into the Craving energy and that their caliber for Having is weak.

The Art of Wooing and Seducing just to arrive at the first act of intimacy is also prone to the hustling energy. Traditionally, men have wooed women. As such, men are prone to becoming skilled hustlers and seducers to get women to say yes. Women in turn understandably become more and more weary and wary, distrusting and cynical about this entire process of being wooed and seduced. They are constantly wondering and calculating whether all the wooing is designed for just the first intimacy alone or is there anything more in it.

## Seduce for the Long Haul

If you are interested in one-time hook-ups and seductions, this book is not for you anyway. My advice is that you not enter into intimate relating lightly, that you postpone oral sex and penetration a decent amount of time and learn to use your hands first. Connect with touch first. If there is real turn-on and resonance in your touch, other forms of sex will be all that much better for it when you get to them.

I teach workshops in pussy-stroking. I encourage my male students to not have oral sex or penetration with a new lover till they have had at least 4 dates of stroking sex, hands-on-genital sex. If things are going well there, if the heat level is so high there that both of you are bursting out of your skin to do other things, then it's a good time to move further.

So as far as the tone and timbre of the initial Wooing & Seduction, instead of promising each other the moon and making vows of eternal passion in order to get someone in bed to have intercourse with them, my recommendation is that people move forward soberly and in broad daylight and take things slowly and really see if there is anything real between them. By the model of the 4 arts of Seduction, woo just enough to get to a SMALL episode of HAVING. If the first experience of Having is worthwhile and both of you want to come back for more, then woo some more to have another episode of Having.

Real Wooing & Seduction is nothing more than making your prospective lover a small offer or invitation they may enjoy saying yes to. I'm personally quite suspicious of any grander gestures of seduction that go beyond such small invitations in the early stages of a relationship.

## Woo & Seduce More as Time Goes By, Not Less

Don't send an expensive gift or 4 dozen long stem roses to a prospective lover you hardly know and are trying to get into bed. Most women I have discussed this subject with have unequivocally expressed that any such grand or lavish gesture from a guy they hardly know makes them feel cautious, not flattered.

Bring the diamond bracelet or the surprise trip to Paris or the dinner at a posh restaurant to the lover who has already enriched your life for a year or two or ten. Show them how much you still enjoy pulling them closer, bridging the gap between the two of you and sweeping them off their feet.


## 2. The Art of Having & Enjoying

This is where it's at! This is where Ecstasy becomes possible. This is where living and loving happens. If this aspect of your relating is happy and thriving, it will contribute a boost to all 3 other aspects of your Desire. If this aspect is a dud, then the game is pretty much over between the two of you. Most of this book is about the art of Having and Enjoying. It's about what gets in the way of Having and Enjoying.

You finally got that person to go out with you; now, how is the date going? Both of you having fun? Glad or delighted to be here? Enchanted and charmed by each

other?  Laughing and giddy in each other's company?
Or are your ass and your feet falling asleep while you
keep stealing glances at your phone or watch?

You've finally gotten the new person in bed.  Now what?
Are you shivering and delighting in each other's touch?
Is the arousal level starting to pour out of your ears?  Or
is your mind noisy with laundry lists and you are hoping
they would stop doing that thing they are doing right
now?

Experience is king here.  How you FEEL is what
matters.  Nothing else will come to the rescue.  It won't
matter how good the person looked on paper or even
how good looking they are.  If you are bored in their
company and their touch leaves you indifferent or
irritated, it's over.  In all the other 3 phases of Desire,
fantasy and imagination can play a prominent and often
misleading role.  But in the phase of Having & Enjoying,
REALITY rules.  If you are not actually able to
experience any enjoyment with this person, nothing can
rescue you.

## Sexual Mastery is Necessary for Having & Enjoying

Lack of skill in this department will help you none. And real skill and confidence will make you very attractive in this phase. If you are consistently able to deliver pleasure and sensation to your partner, if you have the knowledge to handle them and play with them, then the Having & Enjoying can become delightful and nourishing and exhilarating. Remember, Ecstasy lives here! It's only possible when lovers actually meet and touch and interact and move each other's systems. That happens here in the Having & Enjoying. Real skill is needed here to touch Ecstasy. Ecstasy is not an abstract energy. Ecstasy is reached THROUGH the body, not in spite of it. Real knowledge of handling your lover's body is needed. True sexual mastery is needed. One of my desires in writing this particular book is that people will do the preliminary work and then show up for that hands-on education so that they may become amazing lovers. You should be someone who is delightful to get close to, exhilarating and enchanting to have as a lover— someone who is a joy to receive touch from and give touch to.

This is the leaping off point. When the Having & Enjoying works, there are levels and levels of experiences and sensations that are possible between two people.

But there is nothing automatic here, nothing that can be taken for granted. In truth, most relationships falter and fizzle in the Having & Enjoying stage. Most of the time there isn't that much to Have and there isn't much Enjoyment. Often, people feel that the fancy seduction phase with all its promises was too much work for this little pay-off in this phase. It doesn't have to be so. Real Mastery is possible here. But you must seek it.

## 3. The Art of Creating Distance

This is a less understood art. It takes some experience and contemplation to understand its need and its beauty. The first 2 phases we understand more naturally. Desires grip us, infatuation grips us, even by early adolescence we have some experience of wanting someone. That wanting naturally leads to us trying to have them. And trying to have them, at least sometimes, leads to us having them. It's easy to think that this is all there is to the phases of Desire — Feeling the Gap; Closing the Gap.

The Art of Creating Distance from someone you actually desire and want to possess is a more mature art. It takes a little bit of living to realize and appreciate the role it plays in the cycles of Desire.

We want to experience and keep experiencing all the possibilities in Desire:
We want to long for our lover.
We want the experience of coming closer to our lover.
We want the experience of having our lover.
Then, we again want to have the experiencing of longing. Then coming close. Then having. Then longing and wanting and missing and craving. Then wooing and seducing and getting nearer. Then having and ravishing and touching Ecstasy and enjoying and feeling replete and satiated. Then longing.

And for us to have this ongoing dynamic, the art of creating distance after having our lover is a crucial step. Without it, the cycle slows down and stops. Without distance, desire and passion settle down and quieten.

## Eliminate Frivolous Closeness

If you are curled up with your lover on the couch watching TV together, you might be wasting closeness! Are you really relishing the contact with your lover's body?  Is that touch creating a palpable buzz and sweetness in your system and vice versa?  If not, you are wasting Desire Currency!  If your physical closeness is not an active experience of Having & Enjoying each other, then separate!  Create distance instead; it will serve you better in the overall Desire Cycle.

**Sleep Apart!**
Have separate bedrooms.  Most people will sleep better when alone in their own bed.  And that nightly closeness is wasted intimacy.  Keep separate bedrooms.  Keep your own sleeping and waking hours.  Keep your own separate sleeping and waking rituals.  You will be happier to see each other in the morning.

**Allow Each Other to Have Private Lives.**
Even allow each other to have private erotic lives.

**Limit Domesticity.**
If you share a home, domesticity can become a default channel in your communication.  Weed out this tendency.  Limit and bracket domestic life and conversations.

**Cease Information Dumping.**
If you feel part of the joy of having a lover or partner is that you get to come home and tell someone about your

*entire* day, about every bit of office politics and such, you may end up living with a buddy or a roommate rather than a lover after a while. Sharing minutia will sabotage the tension needed for desire.

**Maintain Your Separateness.**
Have your individual interests and pursuits. Keep growing. Stay interesting. When was the last time you surprised yourself? Feeling a little apart from our lover, feeling that he/she is their own person can create that happy tension of distance that inspires Desire.

— — —

# Drama — The Poor Man's Eros

Many couples stumble upon the dynamic of 'make-up sex'. Many couples discover that there can be a short honeymoon period after a fight. Do relationships long enough and you will stumble upon this 3rd principle that some separation and distance is good for Desire.

However, many couples never develop sane and skilled ways of Creating Distance. Instead, they regularly plunge into Drama in order to generate that tension. This is not my recommendation. Drama is cheap and repetitive and ultimately exhausting. And Drama will sabotage any possibility of touching Ecstasy. They are two very different frequencies that live very far away from each other.

So watch out for Drama's pattern. Know the recipe of Drama so you can spot it early. The recipe for Creating Distance through Drama can have one or more of the following ingredients:

- Just start finding your partner wrong.
- Start finding your life wrong and dissatisfying.
- Start sabotaging your partner's self-expression.
- Start blaming your partner for your lack of self-expression and happiness.
- Sulk. Throw tantrums. Be temperamental and make your moods your partner's responsibility.
- Set your partner up to lose.
- Keep changing the rules to keep your lover off-balance.
- All zero-sum games — where if your partner wins, you lose. And vice versa.

## 4. The Art of Remaining an Attractive Shore

There are two challenges about our own attraction that we face in the Desire Cycle:

1. How do I get you to find me interesting, attractive and desirable when you first meet me?

2. How do I get you to KEEP finding me interesting, attractive and desirable after you have already met me and known me for a while?

If we succeed at only the first and fail entirely at the second, the best we can hope for in life is a long series of 1st dates that end in our lovers being disappointed in us. Not a great scenario, obviously.

The second challenge is the true one. The challenge of making desire and attraction and affection last over the long haul is the real thing. It's so much better to hear the story, 'When I first met him/her I didn't really think that much of them. But the more I got to know them, the closer I got to them, the more I saw how interesting, charming, intelligent, sensual and amazing they were.' Compared to hearing, 'Wow, he/she looked so amazing and attractive at first sight, but by the end of the first date I couldn't wait to get away and delete his/her contact from my phone.'

To remain an attractive shore over the long haul, seduce for the long haul. To seduce for the long haul, seduce with the life you are leading.

— — — — — — — — — — — — —

# 8.  Seduce With the Life You Are Leading

There is a deep pessimism underneath our pretending. The premise we are functioning from when we present a false front is: 'As I am, you are not going to like me.'

To build a new relationship out from this core of self-loathing is not ideal architecture.

## Truth In Advertising

Seduction seems to have become a vocation these days. How much time are you spending on social media trying to sound intelligent, caring, spiritual?  How many hours on dating sites?  Advertising your best qualities, polishing that first digital impression, posting that picture taken from just the right angle?

How have the fruits of your labors been?  How are the dates and hook-ups coming along?  Found any lasting friends and lovers?  Made some deep connections?  Had some heart-splitting sex with people you initially found with the flick of a finger?

It is more common for me to hear from someone how she has decided to take a sabbatical from all dating and hookups out of sheer exhaustion and disappointment through our new modality of seduction. What at first appears to be a smorgasbord of sensual and romantic possibilities more often turns into an inner state of contraction, anxiety and failure. People in their 20s are sounding as weary and cynical about romance and relationships as previous generations used to sound at middle age after 3 failed marriages.

What is the flaw in the system?

The flaw is that we are all putting our best face forward. That's the polite version of the answer. The blunt version is: we are all lying. We lie when we seduce. We lie when we have to make a first impression. We lie before and during the first meeting. We are quite capable of lying all through our first sexing!

Our motives for lying are not malicious. We want to be liked. We want to be desired, pursued, accepted. There is nothing wrong with any of these desires. But these very tender desires render us susceptible to presenting a very edited and polished version of ourselves. The result is that the lies we present in order to have someone like us when they first meet us are the same lies that sabotage everything once that relationship proceeds past the initial phase.

The more polished, the more edited our initial presentation to a new lover, the more that relationship will be built on a foundation of quicksand.

## Truth Emerges

Our intimate relationships are the great lie detectors of our lives. Everything that is hidden will be revealed. Everything that is camouflaged will eventually stand naked. Your best first impression will very quickly give way to all those true pieces of yourself that you left on the editing floor while putting together that reel of the 'best of me' for your prospective lovers to see.

When we seduce while wearing a mask, our seduction has no true power or stamina.

The mask will fall in no time. You know why? Because we all know at this point that everyone is wearing a mask! We are all in the mask-presentation business. But we are also in the mask-ripping-away business. We know we are all lying at first! So, as soon as we actually meet, we turn up our lie-detection to the highest setting and try to separate the real from the bullshit in the person sitting across from us. As we should!

We are a people suffocating beneath the weight of our own masks. Appearances and impressions have become all. Instead of presenting an attractive cover for a worthwhile book, we are becoming our covers. It's life according to the gospel of the selfie.

But we keep doing it! We keep looking for that attractive mask. We spend energy getting close to the attractive mask. Then we work hard to rip off the mask. We are disappointed by what we find underneath. We exit. And we start looking for the next attractive mask. You are doing it to them. They are doing it to you. On and on it goes. The only cumulative effect of this cycle is an accumulation of disappointment and disillusionment. We keep feeling cheated by the others because they are wasting our time by lying to us.

Understandably, this is exhausting! I feel exhausted just describing it.

## Person Without Persona

My take on seduction is this: It's always been a rookie mistake to try to seduce with your presentation, your persona. It's terribly shortsighted to try to seduce with a false front. You are not giving any credit to the person you are seducing! Don't you want to seduce someone who is smart enough to figure you out? Don't you want to be with someone sharp enough to separate your brilliance from your bullshit? Don't you want to actually be SEEN by your lover?

That's the stuff that makes the relationship between two people sparkle and buzz over the long run!

But this art of seducing someone by showing them who you really are seems to be quite absent from our current culture. Instead, thanks to the new modalities that technology has offered us for finding prospective lovers, the rookie mistake of seducing with one's persona has gone global. It has become institutional.

Technology dangled a shiny and false possibility in front of us, and we leaped at it! Images. Screens. Soundbites. Quotes. These slivers of information are inherently fallacious, misleading and incomplete. All photographers, filmmakers and editors know this! These tiny bits of abstraction don't represent reality; they distort reality. Ironically, we are all sophisticated enough to know this! And yet, we are not sophisticated enough to NOT keep wagering our hearts and our desires on these slivers of distortion. Predictably, we keep coming up short.

My advice is this: Stop seducing with your Persona. It is an immature and petty way to go through life.

Seduce people with the life you are leading!

In the last chapter I said that there are two challenges we face regarding our attraction:
1. How to attract someone we just met.
2. How to keep attracting that person once we have gotten to know each other.

My suggestion is that you actually NOT have 2 different strategies for these two phases of seduction. In both cases, in both phases: Seduce With the Life You Are Leading!

# A Life Worth Sharing

Are you leading an interesting life? Are you feeling engaged and passionate about how you are spending your days? Are you proud and excited about what you are building here? What skills are you growing? What mastery have you committed yourself to? How are you bringing joy and celebration into your life?

Lead a life that is worth sharing. Lead a life that is worth inviting others into. That invitation to another person to come partake in your genuine life is real seduction.

Creating a rich and engaged life doesn't necessarily mean having a BIG life. What is a big life anyway? Wealth? Big house or fancy car? Some fame and notoriety? None of these need be obstacles to having a meaningful life, but neither are they any guarantees of the meaningful life. Beware of such external markers of success. If you try to seduce with your success or money or material wealth, you have once again slipped into presentation. You are once again holding up your resumé and your markers of success and trying to attract people to those.

The tokens and trophies of success may impress some people, but these are likely to be shallow people who are themselves either looking to just use you for your possessions, or they may be attempting to desperately shore up their own esteem by associating themselves with your trophies.

## Your Internal Life

Here is one of the saddest and truest facts about what happens to a couple by the end of their relationship: One or both people has long stopped finding their partner's internal life interesting!

Think of your last long term relationship. It's very likely that you will find this to be true. Very few people may articulate what they are feeling in these terms: 'I've stopped finding my partner's internal life interesting.' But for our conversation here, it's useful to put it in those terms.

When I hear people talk about why they feel their relationship is done, very seldom is it because, 'my partner is no longer as physically attractive as he/she was when we started.' Even though this insecurity about physical attractiveness is what people tend to fixate on the most. Your partner has not become any less hot. They still possess their degrees, their knowledge, their income, their material possessions. What has changed is that in the beginning you were FASCINATED by them. And this truly means that you were fascinated by their INNER life. And as time went by and you came to know their inner life more completely, you became less and less fascinated by them. You no longer thought too highly about the space your partner occupied within their own head. In fact, by the end of a relationship, most people wish their partner would do anything except insist on sharing one more time what is going on inside their head.

Feeling bored or repelled by someone's inner life also makes for a very powerful anti-aphrodisiac! Do not underestimate the power of inner attraction! If you are with someone who you feel is bright and brilliant and witty and funny and unexpected and enchanting, chances are that liveliness you feel in their company transfers to your lust and your desire for them as well. Feeling drawn in to someone's inner life is a mighty aphrodisiac! It is such a powerful attracter that it can override a dozen other factors — including looks.

So much of what registers as SEXY about a person also emits from their inner life.

We judge the company of others ultimately by this assessment: How do I FEEL after being in this person's company?

Neither good looks, nor any external markers of success will help you at all in this assessment.

Nurturing a rich inner life on the other hand will help you remain that attractive shore that old lovers as well as new ones will want to bridge the gap to in order to get closer to you.


## Your Sexual Mastery Is Genuine Seduction!

Let the journey of your sexual mastery be an integral and ongoing aspect of the life you are creating and leading. True mastery is not about added-on tricks. It's about BECOMING masterful. And pursuit of mastery is an individual affair. It can't be done for someone else — neither to impress them nor to please them or to pacify them. Pursue your sexual expression and mastery because your Eros is an absolutely crucial aspect of YOUR being. Allow yourself to have your individual journey in it. Your partner will merely be the beneficiary of your new mastery.

And allow your partner to have the same journey for themselves. Create the permission field where they too may have the opportunity to explore all the various aspects of their own Eros. Encourage each other's journey towards sexual mastery.

Even when you decide to pursue sensuality training together, try to veer away from the very tempting and common mindset of: 'We are doing this together.' You can certainly be partners in the journey, but have some distance and respect for each other's individual trek. This separation and independence from each other will also help each of you become more of that Attractive Shore to each other.

The more you explore your Eros, even in partnership, the more you are bound to discover how your Eros DIFFERS from your partner's. Allow these differences! Cherish them. Once again, these differences will create that good distance that you will want to bridge. You will keep discovering new facets in your partner to explore and enjoy.

And acquiring real training and skill at moving your lover's system never gets old. That skill gets better in time. It pays high dividends over the long run.

## How to Really Change Your Partner

Since this seems to be an unavoidable pastime of so many people, I would like to propose a better method for going about this hobby: Don't change your partner by attempting to reconfigure them. Change them by inspiring them with the life you are leading. Change them by the choices and decisions you are making. Change them with the way you are pursuing your own desires and ambitions. Be an invitation for them to do the same for themselves.

Try inspiring instead of insisting. And if inspiring them doesn't work, it's very unlikely that the bullying and pleading and complaining will.

## Failure Can Be More Interesting Than a False Mask

If we were to examine this conversation from the perspective of the higher and lower centers, the presentation game doesn't go higher than the 3rd center. It's about looking good and using the other to prop up your own esteem. It's a common enough game, but it is not a modality that connects with Ecstasy. It's a use and be used deal. 'You impress me with your persona baby and I'll impress you with mine. And won't we make a pretty picture together! They will all turn to look.'

As far as Ecstasy is concerned, the pretty cover will help you none. That first impression will help you none. Looking good will help you none. Alas, even being very good looking will help you none. If it did, the best looking people of the world could unite and have the best sex that can possibly be had. But that's a no-go.

On the contrary, your willingness to look bad, to let go, to lose control, to surrender, to take chances, to fail, to fall on your face, to not look like the coolest person in the room may in fact increase the odds of you touching Ecstasy. Letting go of the persona will make you more receptive to higher possibilities.

Our masks are manufactured, maintained, updated and worn at the 3rd center. So if your head is wrapped in a mask, your head ain't going higher than the 3rd center.

Your surface game may work at getting a partner in bed, but your surface game will not take you any further. Convincing a person to have sex with you is one matter, touching Ecstasy together is a whole other journey. And if you are making choices in your seduction that are precluding the possibility of Ecstasy, you are making very poor choices. You are signing up for a life of prolific but mediocre sex.

My encouragement is that you do whatever is within the grasp of your humble humanity to be an invitation for Ecstasy. Being that invitation MATTERS! Your true sexual mastery matters. You being an invitation for your partner's expression and mastery matters. Be THAT person and seduce with that!

The partner who perceives that invitation in you and says yes to that invitation — something real and amazing might be possible with that partner.

— — — — — — — — — — — — —

# 9. Long Term Eros

The 4 arts/principles of desire mentioned in the beginning of this section apply to all relationships at all stages. Learning to use them well for the long term relationship constitutes an art onto itself. If you keep the principles at hand, the theory can illuminate the practice. The principles can help pinpoint where the engine of Eros has stalled and what might be done about it:

1. The Art of Wooing and Seduction.
2. The Art of Having and Enjoying.
3. The Art of Creating Distance.
4. The Art of Remaining an Attractive Shore.

## Fun Before Sex

In a new relationship, sex is fun and fun is sex. For new lovers, to have fun, they have sex. This equation reverses itself in the long term. If a couple isn't having fun, they are not having sex. To have sex, have fun first.

Maybe you have at least one set of friends of this sort — the happy couple! The couple that after a decade or more together still seem to be enjoying each other's company. They are still making each other laugh out loud, playing pranks on each other, taking up new hobbies together every time you see them. Chances are, if you ever went camping or vacationing together with this annoying happy couple, these two are the ones you overheard moaning and groaning after dark, or in the afternoon.

With these happy freaks, it's easy to conclude, 'They are still fucking! No wonder they are still having fun together.' The reality is the other way around: They are still having fun together. And for a long-term couple, that same fun very easily segues into affection and from affection to arousal and sensual play. If a couple is having fun with each other, it's like the lane for the flow of Eros has all green lights. The erotic channel is open and accessible.

And if the couple is NOT having fun together, then we may have one, two or a sea of red lights on that lane of Eros. If you are not having fun together, principle #2 has gone out the window. You no longer have much faith that Having & Enjoying is possible between the two of you.

You might be able to have fun together without moving into Eros in a long term relationship, but having good sex together when you are not having any fun otherwise in each other's company is very difficult.

And let me emphasize that last point — by 'not having fun' I don't mean taking expensive vacations together or going on adventures. I mean not having fun WITH EACH OTHER. Not feeling light and free in each other's company. Not having a clear field between the two of you, a field free of any resentment or held-back communication. I have known well-off couples who live an enviable lifestyle, but they carry their resentments towards each other to their beach house and to their ski chalet.

This state also violates principle #4. If there is a state of displeasure and anger present, you are no longer interested in bridging the gap to your lover. Your lover is no longer an attractive shore to you.

Most long-term relationships that are not thriving are in this state of no-fun, no-sex. The no-fun state usually looks like the weighty silence of resentment that has built up between the two people. Their field is very heavy. The traffic signals are all red inside. Each one is feeling smothered and disempowered or neglected by the other. Why would anyone want to bridge a gap to a person who makes you feel smothered or disempowered or restricted?

If both fun and sex have gone missing from your long term relationship, try to revive the fun first. Put sex on the back burner for now. First clear your highway of love from existing ill-feelings towards each other. That will turn the traffic signals green. An additional skill or two might be needed to get you zooming down that new, open road, but if you have cleared your resentments, at least now that journey would become a real possibility. Trying to get to good sex without clearing your field first, without arriving at a state of some levity in your relating, without first reviving affection between yourself and your partner, is not really possible.

Maybe in some tempestuous, and probably drama-laden, torrid affair you might be able to extract a little bit of good sex with a person you don't have much feeling for, or with a person you actually dislike a bit. Our Eros is rather complex and colorful. Over the short haul, that indifference or dislike might serve principle #3 and evoke desire. But over the long-term, we don't want to fuck people we don't like. And the blunt truth about why many (not all) long term couples are no longer erotic together is because they no longer like each other very much.


## Cleaning House.  Keeping Word.

Long-term relationships are the great crucible of the human experience.  Long term relationships are the ground where we are deeply tested, tried and forged. Learning to 'do' relationships is the primary function of coming here on this human journey.  Any happy and well-functioning long-term relationship deserves high praise.  It is the mark of two grown-ups.  Any two people who are genuinely happy together and there for each other and having fun together deserve high marks!  Even if their erotic life is not spectacular!  Creating a successful partnership, succeeding at working out all the kinks that come along the way over the years—that is an even bigger and more complex accomplishment than building a successful erotic life.  Such a couple has learned the skill of keeping their relationship house clean over the long haul.

There are many factors that might come into the art of keeping a clean relationship house, but there is one that really sticks out for me:  Keeping Your Word!

Without this one element in place, your relationship will surely fail. This is a problem that compounds itself. It's one of those fundamental problems. If this fundamental is not in place, all the other problems get even worse and all the other solutions get weakened and sabotaged. Not keeping one's word while trying to build any relationship over the long run is like trying to build a house on sand or mud. The more pieces you add on, the more precarious the structure will get until it finally collapses.

(Just to be clear and thorough here, I am not saying it's impossible to have good sex with a scoundrel. Many have. Many will. Many are as we speak. Scoundrels can be fun…as long as you don't attempt to civilize them and pull them to the straight and narrow. The conversation here is about long-term eros. Scoundrels aren't good for the long run.)

I often think that all relationship counseling, right from the very first beat, could be commenced in this manner: The counselor sits the couple down on a couch. The first words he/she speaks is: 'Who has not been keeping their word?' Then let both partners scream and yell out their long list of complaints about the other not keeping their word—sort out and organize this list of complaints, address it and keep addressing it until the list is empty and the couple can agree that at least for a month or two, neither has broken their word about anything. Keep digging and get to that stage first before proceeding any further. And if they can't manage to get to that clean slate of 2 people who can trust each other to keep their word, then the relationship is lost. It's pointless to make any other inquiries or offer any other solutions.

## Egalitarianism Is a Bore

#3 is the most common challenge for the long-term relationship. Long term couples are already too close. Egalitarianism is no friend to a couple who are trying to create some good distance between themselves in order to flame the fires of Eros.

The opposite of egalitarianism is POLARITY.

As much as possible, create polarity between yourself and your lover. All the characteristics of your lover that are different from your own make up, cherish them! Emphasize them. Love them. Encourage them. Enjoy them.

Enjoy your differences. Encourage your differences.

Nowhere is this polarity more crucial than in your erotic roles and temperament. Find the differences in your erotic constitution. And, once again, emphasize and cherish and exaggerate those differences. That's where the heat is.

If one of you naturally leans towards being sexually submissive and the other is more dominant, perfect! Consider yourself lucky. The folks who both lean the same way face a bigger challenge! It's much trickier for them to create that good polarity in their Eros.

Incorporating the art of dominance and submission in your erotic dynamic can be a great and lasting boon towards creating a polarity that will keep your sex life sparking over the long run.

Once you have built the dom/sub dynamic in your erotic life, try extending it to other areas of your life. (Seek some mentorship in this area.) It will be challenging and confronting at first for many people. It is not the direction in which our political impetus is right now. But there is something ancient and familiar and even beautiful in such dynamics when you do them consensually and for your own pleasure and get-off. It will feed your erotic energy. Being owned isn't politically fashionable these days, but it can be very hot.

This polarization needs to occur regardless of your gender, your sexual preference and any and all the political heat these days around gender roles. I personally don't care what your sex or your partner's sex is, doesn't matter who is carrying the briefcase and who is baking the soufflé wearing nothing but an apron, I don't care who is being spanked and who is doing the spanking. I don't even care who is being penetrated and who is doing the penetrating—JUST FIND THE POLARITY! Find the good differences between the two of you. In the gap between those differences is where Eros lives.

## Incorporate New-Ass Energy

Examine new-ass energy from the perspective of the 4 principles of desire and it's easy to see why it works, why it can have such a strong erotic charge. We are starting with #4; you see someone who fascinates you, attracts you. #3 is already in place. You can't wait to get to #2. You move forward right away with #1, wooing and seducing.

Who does not wish they can experience again that heat and fascination and that facile Eros they experienced in the first days of their romance? The suggestions in this chapter and book are to help you succeed at that very thing. But one additional way to get to happiness is to directly incorporate new-ass energy into your relationship! Call it Monogamy+. Call it what you want. It works! It can be great. It can be a lot of fun. Not only is it possible to have a lot of fun with a third person you invite into your twosome, doing so can leave a happy charge in your twosome that you can keep enjoying even after the third has left the building.

New-ass energy is a powerful brew. Handle it with care. Put on your radiation suit and your thick gloves and carry the steaming container with respect and caution. The section above on keeping your relationship house clean applies here in spades. If the relationship field in your twosome is not clear, do not head in this direction. If you are harboring resentments, if you feel your partner has been holding you back or has not been listening to you or caring for you, do not head in this direction. Bad things will happen. The container will slip, the green liquid will explode everywhere, and at least one of you will turn into a monster and eat the other.

I separate the relationship journey, the erotic journey into two broad sections:

1. Going from Bad to Good.
2. Going from Good to Better.

New-ass energy applies only to the second journey. If you are trying to go from bad to good, start by communicating, by cleaning up your resentments, by starting to keep your word, by learning new sensuality skills.

If you have already done all that, if you are already having fun together and enjoying each other and enjoying at least a modest amount of joy in your sexual relating, then playing with a third can be a delightful and successful expedition.

Bring the clear communication that exists between the two of you to your visiting guest. Make sure everyone is on the same page regarding boundaries and desires. Where in doubt, OVER-COMMUNICATE. When in doubt, do less sexually rather than more.

Once you have set your agreements and boundaries, DO NOT change or renegotiate them during the scene (except to speak your limits in real time and end the scene EARLY if it is not feeling good). Better to end on a happy and friendly note.

The wisdom of Seducing With The Life You Are Living applies here deeply. Build a happy life and dynamic into which you might invite a third. The logic, the preparation, the execution of such an encounter is fundamentally not all that different from inviting someone over for a dinner date. Be gracious hosts. Be happy hosts. Make sure you like your guest and your guest likes you. Let your guest know what you will be serving. Cook something that both you and the guest enjoy.

If you have gained competence at the art of creating win-win scenes and scenarios with your primary lover, it's a shorter leap ahead to design a win-win-win scene with a visiting lover.

Our Eros is complex. Even with the best and most loving of partners, we can't fully learn about our make up, our desires, our capacities. Successfully making room for a third can not only be fun, it can be revelatory.

## Seek Sexual Self-Expression. Not Sex.

How is your sexual journey going? What is it that wants to open up next in your erotic expression? What is unfolding in your erotic archetypes? What do you want to explore next in your Eros?

The key words in this inquiry are: YOU & YOUR.

Separate yourself from your partner and make this solitary inquiry. Try to abandon the idea of 'Our Sex Life.' This idea is a fiction. There has never, ever been such a thing as 'Our Sex Life' for anybody.

Each person's erotic journey is their own. Each person's Eros is in flux.

A big aspect of being a competent lover is granting yourself as well as your partner this independence and this respect for their erotic constitution and erotic journey. Part of being a good lover is perceiving where your partner is erotically and seeing how you might meet them there and engage them there.

'Our Sex Life' is a lazy and half-assed idea. It's an excuse to show up sexually unprepared and sexually unqualified to your lover. The sum ends up being smaller than the individuals in this equation.

You want to know what makes for a great sex life between two people? TWO GREAT LOVERS! Two people who individually are great lovers. Two people who are present in their body and in their touch. Two people who like each other and are skilled at handling each other's bodies. Two people who understand Eros enough to empathize with their partners and evaluate their needs and desires and turn-ons and sexual archetypes.

Two people who have been passionately pursuing their own Erotic Self Expression. Two people who have a genuine desire to be good lovers and have thus spent time and energy acquiring knowledge and skills that allow them to be good lovers.

In the absence of this paradigm of Erotic Excellence, what most couples fall back on is a very meager yardstick of what constitutes a good or successful sex life. The most common couples' complaint is that they are not fucking enough. Intercourse becomes the measure for what sex is. It has the added illusion of an 'us activity'. It's easy to confuse penetration sex as a marker for 'Our

Sex Life'. It's a bad marker. Not only is penetration or intercourse a very small portion of a thriving and rich sex life, even the premise that fucking/intercourse is an 'us' activity is inaccurate! In truth, more often than not, lovers are having very different experiences within their own bodies even during intercourse. It's just that most people lack the awareness as well as the language and communication to articulate this fact to each other. Or, in most cases, they are too afraid to inquire that deeply into sex, fearing they are not going to like the information that surfaces as a result of such inquiry.

Your Eros is BIG. Your erotic journey is a real and true aspect of your soul journey. The reason so many people are living in such high levels of frustration and disappointment in their sex is because they have relegated their own Eros to second-class status in their lives. You have taken a BIG part of yourself and tried to shove it into a small and manageable box in your life. By the standards of what good Eros looks like in our current, impoverished sexual culture, even if you succeed at sex, you don't really end up feeling like a success. Even if you succeed at being good looking and attracting lots of lovers and having lots of intercourse, you are likely to feel in your soul that the whole affair seems to be a lot of fuss for too little pay off. And you are right!

By the popular standards of a good sex life, even to win is to not really win all that much.

But the fault is in us. Most people have set their sights too low. Most of us have shortchanged our erotic selves. Most of us have traded our erotic journey for conquest and numbers and notches and a few sex acts.

Build more respect for your erotic self. Build more respect for your lover's erotic expression. Acquire the skills to engage and delight in your own complexity and your lover's complexity. Your long-term Eros will benefit. And from that wider perspective, Ecstasy is accessible.

— — — — — — — — — — — — —

# JOURNEY

# 10. Your House Is Not Secure

Success makes cowards of us all.

That sounds a bit judgmental. Let me back up. What prevents us from new experience is fear of loss. If you feel a new force in life tugging at you, but you remain reluctant to explore it, it's fear that's holding you back. If you feel inspired to try something new, but feel immobilized by some inner force that won't let you say yes to the new inspiration, it's the fear that the new will come at a cost of something that you have acquired in life.

The more you have, the more you have to lose, and the greater this fear of loss. The bigger this fear of loss, the less open you will be to inspiration, to exploring new directions.

Why does that matter in the sensual realm? Because the thing about most folks who have managed to build successful lives is that they have not included sexual self-expression in their castle. You may be a good wife or husband, a dutiful parent and child, a successful employee or entrepreneur. You have a beautiful home and savings, you are respected and liked, you have a filled calendar. You may have even managed to add a few items to your life that generate mild envy in your acquaintances. Well and good. But chances are, given our culture, your sexual self-expression is not one of these coveted items.

So now what do we do? It may seem easy to say "I'll just add sex now." But I've seen over the years that it's not so simple. The hard wiring that got you to success also contains some very effective mechanisms to sabotage your sexual expression. Your success will often keep you from seeking your sexual mastery. Best to be aware of this equation and what that means for you.

## Success's Imperative Is Retention.

Once you get it, you want to hold on to it. Once you've acquired it, you don't want to lose it. That would be going backwards. That would be failure. So success says, 'Get more if you can, but don't give anything up in return.' Get more! That's the idea. Keep adding.

As far as the growth of material possessions is concerned, this logic often works. Upgrade! Newer phone. Promotion. Better car. Bigger house. A more lavish vacation this year because business has been good.

Nothing wrong with any of this. That's why the decisions are not hard to make. There is no fear of loss. Quite the opposite. You are preparing your bragging rights when such expansion happens in your life.

But not all expansion fits this bill. You can't add more of something you've never had in your life. And there are things worth having that require a wager. They cannot be purchased outright. They may require a sacrifice. They may demand that we relinquish a hard-earned success.

Sexual expression is one of these difficult items. There isn't any inherent nobility in this. There isn't any essential reason that this needs to be so. It's just a fact of our culture and our world. Proper sexual expression is taboo. It is not respectable. It does not fit in our life. When the *NY Times* starts publishing an EROS section right next to its Food and Style section, you will know this is changing. But such a change is nowhere in sight, not even in the most permissive and tolerant pockets of the world. In our Eros, in this tremendously important segment of our life, our soul is still living a banished existence. The message we get is clear: you are on your own if you want to go into this exploration. And you

better be careful.  Because if you are not, it will cost you.
It will cost you your success.

Here are some of the ways this equation plays out:

## The Young Seek It

The young have less to lose.  They have not accumulated
much success yet.  Their failures and experiments are
more readily forgiven by their elders.  Kids experiment.
Kids fool around.  Kids rebel.  So, youth is granted
greater permission for sexual expression.  This is not
bad.  But it's not great either.  Trouble with the young is
they don't know anything.  They are unformed and
uninformed.  They lack maturity for truly touching
Ecstasy.  Their foundations are still shifting and fickle.

It would be another matter if this exploration began in
youth and continued to mature into adulthood.  But
mostly this does not happen.  The sexual expression gets
abandoned once adult life and the pursuit of worldly
success commences.  The first year undergraduate may
be full of verve for redefining her or his romantic relating
and sexing, but the first year law student has already
settled down and is looking around for a sensible spouse.

The first year associate is very much on the straight and narrow. The first year partner is all but staid.

The exuberance, the curiosity does not grow with the years. So, in essence, the expression of youth ends up being an incomplete and immature journey. This ever-continual abandonment of sexual expression as a life-long unfolding keeps it from reaching a level of legitimacy and sophistication that it truly deserves. Without reaching such levels, the *Times* will never consider starting an Eros section and giving erotic recommendations for the mid-winter weekend next to their fine recipe for squash soup that goes well with a certain Riesling.

## The Disillusioned Seek It

When the 30 year marriage has collapsed, the kids are gone, the charm of youth has started to dissipate in the reflection in the mirror, sexual expression ends up on people's bucket list. They come to it after the closing bracket of their middle years, after the notion that they have built a successful life begins to crumble a little.

It's fine as far as that goes. Start seeking it at 50 or 60. Better late than never.

The late starters come with a mix of their strengths and weaknesses. Often they know well who they are. They are more settled in their foundation; this supports their journey. They can be fast learners, like smart kids playing catch-up in a subject they suddenly realize they forgot to study.

Just as often, the passing of years has created an accumulation of shame and repression that now burdens the middle-aged shoulders. A lot of clearing needs to happen before any new adventures can truly start.

These older, influential players are often so successful in the world that they know they can take on this new adventure without having their work, their life, their legacy be damaged by it. They have enough mettle, enough gravitas, and enough power and prominence such that they can push back on judgments that the world may pass on them.

Moreover, the folks in this group tend to be ultra-discrete. They choose to not make their sexual journey a public matter. They use their resources to create a private world of exploration. They create a haven for themselves that remains isolated and insulated from mainstream culture. They split their persona — public and private. They have become too pragmatic and savvy by middle age to take unnecessary gambles.

## The Inspired Adventurers Seek It

That would be me. And others of my ilk. Folks who never thought this is what they would be doing when they grew up. Who found their way into this sphere by some stroke of providence. Many in this category started out just to make improvements in their own lives. Along the way they discovered that they actually might be a bit gifted in this realm. They feel inspired to create a proper and enriched sensual life. Some found a sense of community among their co-seekers. Some have become teachers.

## More Than Half the Globe CAN'T Seek It!

They can't truly pursue sensuality work because doing so would have dire consequences to their life and liberty from the oppressive regime and culture they reside in. They are essentially omitted from this conversation. We will always choose survival over anything else, including self-expression.

## Then There Are the Rest of You Who Don't Seek It

The successful ones. The sensible ones. The ones still busy with the upgrade life. You are the bulk of the population—ones who have the liberty to seek sexual self-expression, but choose not to.

You are the real revolution waiting to happen. You are the ones in whom Ecstasy continues to lay dormant, waiting and waiting in Casablanca because you make no effort to go anywhere. You probably don't even believe in Ecstasy. It's not a priority for you. Not enough to wager your successes.

Success's imperative is retention. Genuine sexual expression in our culture can come at a huge cost.

## What Have You Got To Lose?

1)   Your Respectability.
2)   Your Stability.
3)   Your Identity.

No wonder most people never begin the path towards sexual education and mastery! This is a high price to pay indeed. Let me offer you some thoughts on these three Fears of Loss. I have seen enough of you who do make the leap. I've made such a leap myself. So I have some observations and advice on these three fears. They are legitimate fears. The loss is real. So the fear of loss is reasonable and logical.

## Your Respectability

My advice is very pragmatic—do your best to not wager it! Seek your education on the down-low. You don't need to advertise what you are doing. Your neighbors and your friends don't need to know what you are up to. They in fact don't WANT to know what you are up to. You don't need to tell everyone about the latest sex workshop you signed up for on social media. No need to post an image of your lover in bondage rope even though you are very proud of your new rope skills.

Discretion is not shame. It is a largely necessary tool to address legitimate fears of loss.

Women especially need to take this route. Men enjoy greater permission for sexual expression than women. The fear of losing one's respectability is much greater for women. So create a private life.

## Your Stability

This is a bigger challenge. The common scenario regarding coupledom that shows up on my couch in coaching sessions or in my workshops is this: One person in the coupledom is ready to go forward and the other isn't. One person is ready to do something about creating a richer erotic life, and the other is ambivalent and would like to continue in the status quo. One partner has discovered her turn-on with kink and Dominance & Submission and the other is afraid to venture in.

The stability of the relationship is threatened. The couple doesn't know where or how they will end up if they seek some new paradigms, if they allow their dormant dom/sub archetypes to come forth and have expression.

Frankly, I have never had a good solution for couples in this department. I have no way of guaranteeing the continuation of their coupledom. In fact, I tell people I cannot promise that they will not grow further apart as a result of seeking sensual education.

The only thing to point out to people regarding the fear of loss of stability is this: You are kind of screwed already. If you have reached the level of dissatisfaction where you cannot abide by your status quo, then what choice do you have at this point anyway? Your frustration and disappointment levels are already high. If you continue as you are, chances are your relationship will disintegrate anyway. And on its slow path to disintegration, you will only accumulate more resentment and disappointment towards each other. One partner will feel the other is holding him/her back. The other partner may feel like a failure. It's a terrible way to keep going. So might as well take a plunge forward and see what comes.

This bind that couples end up in is a natural outcome of trying to build a successful life while omitting a crucial aspect of our being from the blueprint of that life. Our Erotic Self-Expression is not a small matter. Our success in ignoring this self-expression for decades does not diminish the call in our soul that we are missing a crucial component of our journey, that we have been cheated out of one of our birthrights.

I see couples who have succeeded in building a great home, family and security, but they have left out erotic self-expression. Now, trying to insert this rather large piece back into their life is threatening to dismantle the edifice they have built together. This is bound to be so. This is analogous to building a beautiful brick mansion from which you omit a crucial room—you build your mansion and never put in a kitchen or a bathroom or a bedroom. Now, when you suddenly realize you need to cook or bathe or sleep, it dawns on you that you may have to tear the whole thing down to insert the needed room you forgot to include initially.

## Your Identity

This is the biggest hurdle of them all. The title of this chapter refers to this aspect more than the others discussed so far. More than the real houses that we construct as our life progresses, the most stubborn and precious construction we undertake is of our identity. Our self-image. Who I think I am. And the most common resistance to the call of Ecstasy and what it would require of you is, 'That's just not who I am.'

Moving towards Ecstasy, toward erotic self-expression, will indeed shift your notion of who you are. This is the other renovation that is going to happen in your life — that of your identity. And we hate change in our identity more than any other change. And we fear a threat of change to our identity more than the loss of our material wealth.

This portion of the journey is the most personal one. It really is a matter between you and your soul. I personally try not to engage people in this level of their struggle—simply because it takes so much energy. I'd rather teach people who have crossed this hurdle for themselves and are ready to learn.

The wisdom that is needed in this aspect is the same wisdom that is needed to tend to our soul overall. Seek within. Seek wisdom and guidance from the sources that you trust. My two cents for you in this area are written in the title of this chapter: Your House is Not Secure. As desperately as we spend this life building the mansions of worldly security and personal identity, all of it is a construct. All of it will crumble in the end.

There are aspects of our soul that need expression during this earth journey. Have some respect for that expression. Give it room. Let the yearnings of your soul trump your constructs. That's where discovery is. That's where Ecstasy becomes possible.

— — — — — — — — — — — — — —

# 11. The Perils of Expansion

Who doesn't want expansion? More freedom? A greater range for feeling and acting in the world? Change Change Change! Change for the better! The new me! More loving. Less held back. Faster & lighter.

Expansion needs to come with a few warning signs. That's what this chapter is about.

## Our System Is Elastic!

We hardly ever have an experience of expansion without our system recoiling into a contracted state soon after. Our soul expanding is not like adding length to a thread; it's like stretching a rubber band. There are existing forces in our system that are standing in opposition to the current expansion that is happening. Something new comes in our life — we hear a new teacher or idea that inspires us, we encounter a practice that offers us a new way of being — well and good. The new prompts the expansion. But don't underestimate the old. The old that is in us will pull back and try to reinstate its stasis.

Expansion is not an event.  Expansion is a process.  It is a tug of war between the new and the old.  And the two forces spring back and forth for a while before a new equilibrium is arrived at.

And the new does not always win.  Often times, the new fails several times initially.  Most of us reject our epiphanies the first time.  Often, our epiphanies have to come knocking a few times before we yield.  Sometimes people pay their therapist money for 3 or 4 years just to dig down and unearth the epiphany they had 3 or 4 years ago.

The New Comes.  The Old Recoils.  When this recoiling event takes place, if we are not aware of the elastic nature of our system, we can end up in a lot of confusion.  Expansion feels great!  But when the recoil sets in, we can lose faith in the newfound expansive element.  The initial high of the epiphany leaves us.  It is replaced by fear and doubt.  The fear makes wrong the new event; it declares it a sham, a delusion.  In an attempt to restore order, our mind retorts: 'Reality is HERE, where it's always been, all that new stuff is just nonsense.'

The contraction phase can even turn violent and combative.  Those whose ideas and visions our current world is built upon, many of them we threw stones at when they first proposed those ideas. Our track record in this area is not great. When we look back on the journey of our soul, some of the most embarrassing moments we spot are such events when we slammed the door on a genuine opportunity or invitation.

## Addition vs. Reconfiguration

In the material world, change commonly takes the form of ADDITION. The answer to , 'What's new?' is generally a list of things or experiences that we have added to our life since the last time we were asked that question. We talk about the new phone or car, the most recent vacation or adventure.

Expansion in our soul journey, in our self-expression, is not an addition; it is a RECONFIGURATION. An existing part of us gets yanked out and disassembled. Something new and unprecedented gets constructed in its place.

Addition is easy. Reconfiguration hurts!

## Reconfiguration = Destruction + Creation

It's the Destruction part of the process that hurts! Addition is as painless as shopping. Reconfiguration is a crucible. A little death has to precede the creation of our new self. The bigger the reconfiguration, the bigger will be the old part of us that gets knocked down.

Sensual self-expression has been on the back burner for most people. So, expansion in this area of our constitution is particular susceptible to the pain of reconfiguration. Expect to face inner battles with your shame! Expect your older identity to put up a big fight. There are many old voices that reside in this part of your house. They won't leave the first time you ask them to.

The characters in fables have to go through trials and make sacrifices in order to succeed at their mission. These trials and sacrifices are the outward representation of inner destruction. Without the painful destruction element, there would be no 'journey' in the Hero's Journey.

## Your Expansion Will Disturb Others

The people who are in your life right now might not FIT in your life once the expansion occurs!

Imagine a formed jig-saw puzzle. Now imagine that one of the pieces from the middle of the puzzle stands up, shakes itself off and changes its shape a bit.

Your expansion will 'rub' the people around you. And they may or may not be onboard with your change.

For me, the test of a great relationship is how well the two people are an invitation for each other's expansion.

## Women First

In just about all the couples I encounter in my work, this reconfiguration is first occurring in the women. Women are the ones requesting or demanding an expansion in their sensual life. Women are the ones proposing a shift in the relationship dynamics. And their long-term partners or husbands are in deep reluctance regarding these new demands.

The most common coaching request I get from women is, "How do I get my man to be more dominant in the bedroom?" The response I get from their men to this request is, "This is not the woman I married! This is not the agreement we had. I am a nice guy. I treat her well.

I don't screw around. But now, she wants me to be an entirely different person and treat her in a way that I have been taught all my life is NOT how a man is supposed to treat a woman. This is not fair!"

Women are expanding. Men are struggling to make themselves bigger to make room for that expansion.

And the Journey is not always successful. Often times the coupledom doesn't survive the expansion. And, understandably, the couple sometimes choose their stability over their expansion.

## Expansion Shifts Our Modus Operandi

Inner expansion shifts our outer methods and approaches to sex and relating.

We have many behaviors and ways-of-being that we are operating with. Many of these will stop fitting with the new you.

How do you seduce? By playing the cute one? The flirty and innocent one? The aloof one? The unattainable one? The smart yet sexy one?

How do you get your way with people? How do you respond to being challenged? To being complimented? To limitation?

How do you go about getting your desires met? Are you direct? Coy? Aggressive? Passive?

We are ingenious creatures. We have a million adaptations we have made in response to the world we have faced, the challenges we've had to overcome. And we are heavily laden with ways of being that have worked for us in the past. These ways of being are part of our inner structure.

When the reconfiguring of our being happens, some of these ways of being get knocked down. Some of our Modus Operandi ends up in the rubble, in the recycle pile.

This can be a bit disorienting. It's like we had a particular skill until just yesterday, but it is gone today. You find yourself in a relearning phase within a familiar section of your life. And the new way of being carries different resonance.

Almost always, this shift in sexual attitude moves in the direction of more directness and more honesty. If you were coy before, after a phase of genuine expansion, you may find yourself being shockingly blunt in your requests and communication with a lover. You may no longer be able to tolerate bad sex. You are likely to become less polite when a lover is being sloppy or unconscious.

If you find yourself staring in the mirror and asking, 'Who the hell is this person?', that's a good sign.

These shifts make possible new actions and new kinds of relationships. New directions in our journey open up. We become capable of creating things in our life that were out of reach before the shift.

Accomplishing the unprecedented requires that we engage our life in an unprecedented manner. For that to happen, reconfiguration has to occur in our emotional make up — that is essentially what 'Expansion' is: a reconfiguration of our emotional make up.

## Forgiveness as a Yardstick of Expansion

When in doubt, Forgive! It's worth a decade of therapy.

Forgiveness IS expansion.

Forgiveness is destruction! It is the destruction of an old and malignant structure in our system. It is an exorcism of sorts. The exit of the old ghosts creates room for new construction.

If you are feeling emotionally stuck and stifled in your life, look and see how many people you can forgive. Forgiveness is like spring cleaning for the soul.

True forgiveness will demand that you take on more in life. The space it creates leaves us wondering, 'Now what?' What am I going to do with all this space in my emotional life? When we stop complaining about something, all of a sudden we have a lot more time on our hands.

The decluttering that forgiveness creates in our soul becomes a passage for Ecstasy.

— — — — — — — — — — — — — —

# 12. D/S Training for Everyone

D/S. BDSM. B for Bondage. D for Discipline. S for Sadist. S for Sex. S for Satisfaction. D for Dominance and Dungeon and Determined, Doggie, Deviant, Devastating. M for Leopold von Sacher-Masoch. M for Marquis de Sade. No wait, that's S! V for Variety and Veracity and V shapes in the air made by legs and heels. B for Bondage. B for Bee and you Bet your ass.

## What Is Kink anyway?

How about it's me putting some 3/4" nylon rope around your wrists real quick, yanking the rope and your wrists up and above your head, pushing you back against the wall, holding you pinned there and then just… placing soft kisses on your cheeks. And occasionally biting down on your ear?

How about you handcuffing your man to the radiator, having him naked and helpless on his back as you light a 3"X9" pillar of dripping candle. Then you proceed to suck his cock at a slippery, leisurely pace till it feels he is close to his edge and then you grab that candle that has been accumulating melted wax and you drain that wax on your man's chest making him squeal in pain and surprise; you see him arch his back up in the air, but his cock starts to lose steam. The pain is too much. So you have him settle down a bit, soothe his shock and then start on his cock again till it is up to the tipping point and then again grab the waiting, dripping wax?

Or is it having your partner slap your ass or your face when you know you are getting close to climax. Why? Because you simply know that it works. It does something. It makes the pussy throb harder and does the same to the cock. So, 'hit me. Slap me! Spank me! Harder!'

Or is it putting on a strap-on and fucking your man in the ass?

Or is it getting or giving a good flogging?

Or a stiff caning?

Cattails?

Suspension?

A little water sport? To mark your lover as your property?

Dressing in drag and fucking a gender you usually don't?

Getting tied up intricately and getting fed strawberries?

Getting tied up intricately and getting slowly eaten out? Then fucked?

Getting tied up intricately and being walked around a party, getting shown off to strangers?

Getting tied up intricately in really thin rope so you can get dressed to the nines on top of it and go to the opera all abound up inside?

What is kink?

Licking your lover's asshole?

And enjoying it?

NOT enjoying it but doing it as consensual punishment for something you did?

Enjoying being called a whore during sex?

Enjoying being humiliated?

Enjoying dressing up as a pony and having your lover ride you around?

Enjoying going out in public without panties because your Dom commanded you to do so for his amusement, and you live to please your Dom?

What is Kink?

Anal sex? Threesomes? Orgies? Suspension rigs? Degradation Play? Orgasm Control? Spreader Bars? Nipple Clamps?

The clever answer would be, 'It's everything I've always wanted to do but have been too chickenshit or lazy to try.'

Kink is 8000 varieties of Erotic play. And those 8000 flavors are for YOU!

Kink is not compensation. Kink is not deviance. Kink is not just for the kinky. If it is, then we are all kinky. Kink is imagination. Kink is sensual creativity. Kink is bringing a gourmand's palate and discernment to Eros.

Kink is sexual mastery. Kink is appreciation for the depth and complexity of our human desires. Kink is play. Kink is deeper penetration—into our longing, into our get off, into our Ecstasy.

So my whole-hearted recommendation is that you get kinky fast. Expand your palette. Do one or two things you have longed to do for a long time — things you know will generate a genuine turn-on and erotic expression for you —things that you've just been too afraid to try because of your fear or your self-image or your blah blah blah.

Seek training. Seek mentorship. Watch others do it. Ask for advice. Make friends. Find community. Acquire Mastery. Become Kinky—with skill and style.

We are suffering from imagination hypoxia in our erotic life.

Seek training in the darker arts because those arts are for YOU! It's where the oxygen is for your sexual expression.

## Dominance & Submission vs. Kink

I want to draw a very basic map for you for this terrain. For the uninitiated, any play that involves Dominance and Submission is kinky. Rope bondage is kinky. Spanking is kinky, so is dripping wax on your lover and wearing a leather corset and a million other joys. Casually speaking, this is all true. But there is a basic structure to this dynamic: All flavors of kink occur under the partnered dynamic where one person is embodying the DOMINANT archetype and the other person is embodying the SUBMISSIVE archetype.

D/S is the overarching structure under which all kink thrives.

What is a Dominant/Submissive dynamic?

Any form of relating that involves some transfer of power between two parties is a Dom/Sub dynamic.

D/S dynamic is a polarized dance. Two people come and play complimentary roles — not unlike in ballroom dancing.

Let's use Ballroom dancing as an analogy for this structure; it fits quite well. Ballroom dancing in itself has a certain structure. Ballroom dancing implies two dancers doing a partnered dance. It implies that one person leads; the other follows. It implies a starting position of palm in palm, other hand on hip and shoulder.

If you go deeper into the structure of ballroom dancing, you will discover that there are other protocols and imperatives in place — such as, one of the jobs of the leader is to show off the follower! The man is there to make the woman look good.

These are all parameters for Ballroom Dancing itself. But under the umbrella of Ballroom Dancing, there are MANY different dances. A couple can dance a tango or foxtrot or salsa or swing or mambo or samba or waltz and many more.

All the various dances are flavors of KINK. But they all take place, they all shine, they all thrive under the structure and protocol of the Dom/Sub dynamic between two people, where one person takes the lead and the other surrenders and follows.

## Learn the Steps and Come to the Ball!

Learn to Dom and learn to Sub. This is a very rich terrain. It will open up your erotic possibilities. It will allow you to have experiences that simply cannot be had solo or within an egalitarian dynamic. It will give you access to parts of your psyche that have been laying dormant. It will show you new ways to come into your body, to say yes to your desires, to find acceptance for your erotic make up. It can show you how to access internal spaces ranging from peaceful and grounded to thrilling and on the verge of overwhelm.

If all that is not motivation enough, acquiring knowledge and skill in the D/S realm can even enrich non-erotic components of your life. It can provide you with skills you can employ in your work and your leadership. It can help you have a clearer relationship to the planet and your responsibilities in it. It might even have something to contribute to your family and parenting life. And it can provide an opening in your spirituality and in your relationship to whatever higher power you believe in.

I've used D/S training to help actors reach a new level of depth in their craft. I've trained people in D/S so they can act in a more empowered and enlightened way with difficult bosses or parents. I've seen D/S training bring an overall life clarity to people when all that they were initially seeking was to spice up their marriage. I've seen long-term couples go from patterns of bickering and mutual sabotage to a D/S dynamic that is replete with skilled and elegant relating and sensuality.

Before you plunge into any particular dance of kink, before you take up rope play or spanking or any other varieties I listed at the top of this chapter, learn the fundamentals first. First and foremost, learn to Dom and learn to Sub. And some training is needed to acquire this art.

We all have a visceral understanding of what NONCONSENSUAL domination and submission is. Every headline in every newspaper on every single day is pretty much a story of nonconsensual domination and submission. What the structure and protocol of CONSENSUAL domination and submission is requires some learning and mentorship. Consensual domination and submission is anchored in two people giving each other what they truly want. It is anchored in creating games and making agreements in which both parties win. It is anchored in affection and love between two people. It is anchored in two people wanting greater expression and joy for each other. Consensual Domination and Submission in fact has a higher standard for how two people need to show up for each other if they are to do this dance well. They have to be in a deeper state of agreement. They need to communicate more and better. They need to be skilled at playing their roles individually, and they need to be invested in their partner doing well because the two of you are on the same ride.

## Contempt Before Investigation

D/S play is an area laden with misconceptions and bad information. Popular media has long depicted D/S relating in severely distorted ways. Most of the time they are not depicting CONSENSUAL D/S dynamic at all. They are generally depicting an unhealthy, nonconsensual dynamic that is dressed in leather and stilettos.

There is a common piece of advice given to writers, 'Write what you know.' When I see D/S portrayed on TV and in movies and even in many books, I can tell that the writer knew crap about what he/she was writing about when it comes to consensual D/S play. This bad representation of D/S applies also to some very popular books that many of you have read—books that purported to depict consensual Dominance & Submission, but were severely off the mark in doing so.

So people are burdened with a lot of bad notions of what this realm is. Unfortunately, it is one of those topics that people think they know, but in fact do not. As a result, many never get around to knowing it for real. This area suffers gravely from the attitude of 'contempt before investigation'.

I'll repeat this point: All of us know what NONCONSENSUAL Domination and Submission looks like. The history of humanity is nothing other than a history of nonconsensual domination and submission. But what CONSENSUAL D/S is, very few of you have understood and explored.

So my encouragement to you is, come investigate. Put aside any images of people being led around on dog collars. Not that there is anything wrong with having your lover on a leash. But put aside the bad, scary, absorbed-from-TV-notions that are keeping you from actually learning and playing and discovering.

# Why Surrender?

Because there are some very rich experiences to be had in life that can only be had when you surrender. There is a lot that we can do for ourselves. But there is a whole lot more that becomes possible only when we hand ourselves over to a partner. You can't give yourself the experiences of being tied up and handled. You can't give yourself the experience of being pampered or attended to. You can't give yourself the experience of being pushed to your limits. You can't tease yourself, surprise yourself, take yourself out of control, feel at the mercy of.

You need another. And in this dance with the other, you need to learn how to take charge and how to surrender. You need to learn the art of taking over somebody's system and you need to learn to give it up to your partner.

The trouble with most people in the world today is they are unskilled at both of these positions. Most people are lousy at both taking control as well as at giving up control. Most people don't want to assume that big position in which their partner can feel held and thus surrender, and we are unskilled at the art of letting go and trusting and handing ourselves over to our lover.

Instead of floating through the ballroom as two skilled and practiced dancers, most lovers are continually tripping on each other's feet, never able to resolve what the dance is, what each of their steps are, or who is leading and who is following.

Egalitarianism is wonderful in the political and social realm. We do need equality there. We do need to continue the work of eradicating nonconsensual Domination and Submission from the world.

But at the same time, consensual Domination and Submission is an art form that is direly needed in intimate relationships these days. And mind you, there is no agenda here on who plays what part—what gender, what position, etc. Just learn to skillfully Dom and skillfully Sub. It will open up new dimensions in your life. It will give you access to experiences that are too rich and delightful to forego on the human journey. It will open up many chambers of your Eros. It will open up paths to Ecstasy.

— — — — — — — — — — — — —

# SURRENDER

# 13.  Receptivity

How you show up in a relationship matters.  Your attitude towards your partner is a decisive factor in how your relationship is going to turn out.  Your Receptivity towards your partner will determine how deeply they are able to penetrate your heart and sex, how deeply they are able to get to know you and contribute to your happiness and expression.

It's easier to focus on the attitudes and shortcomings of others.  This conversation is about turning the focus on one's own Receptivity.  There are many factors that influence our Receptivity.  At the basic level of Receptivity Influences: If you are tired or cranky, your Receptivity will be low; if you are angry or distracted, the same contraction will occur.  On the other hand, if you are well-rested and in a good mood, you will be more receptive to just about everyone, including your lover.

The rest of this chapter is about a few big influencers of Receptivity that are less obvious.

## Esteem & Receptivity

Those we consider of high esteem, we open ourselves up to — we are receptive to them. Those we consider lower in esteem, we shut down our receptivity to.

Think of the last time you felt snubbed by someone. You might have been at a party or a work meeting or a dinner where there were strangers at the table. The person you felt snubbed by either avoided eye contact and conversation with you entirely, or they seemed in a hurry to take their attention away from you when you were speaking. The feeling we get when this happens is: This person is declaring, "You are not worth knowing. My attention is wasted on you." If your perceptions in such an instance are on target and not merely a projection of your insecurities, then you are correctly perceiving that the snubbing person's reluctance to put attention on you, their lack of receptivity towards you, is an indication that they have evaluated your social worth and found it to be lacking.

Compare that unhappy experience to the opposite kind. Think of a time when you had the chance to meet someone you admire, someone you hold in high esteem. Think how open and eager and receptive you felt to meet them, to listen to them, to engage them. And if they seemed to like you also or if they laughed at your joke, think how incredibly good it felt that *this* extraordinary person was finding *you* interesting.

This connection between Esteem & Receptivity is logical and efficient. Our time and attention are limited. Why should we put attention on people and things that are not worth our time? Why should we be receptive to people who are a bore, or people we have no desire to get to know?

This Esteem-Receptivity equivalence plays out in intimate relationships in many ways. The higher you esteem your partner, the more you will be receptive to them. If bad feelings accumulate between the two of you, and your partner starts to fall in your esteem, your receptivity will close down towards him or her. The bouquet of flowers they bring you today will please you less than the one they brought when you thought better of them. Their sexual advances will thrill you less if your receptivity to them has closed due to recent conflict or hurt.

The less you Respect your partner, the more that aperture of Receptivity will close inside you towards your partner. The closed receptivity will limit the depth of your sensual relating.

Another correlation between Esteem & Receptivity shows up in how well we think of ourselves. If you are in the doldrums about your own worthiness, your receptivity will shut down. If you are feeling unattractive or unlovable, it will be very difficult for a lover to get through to you. Your castle gates are shut, alligators in the moat. It can be quite exhausting work to try and give to someone who is not interested in receiving.

This type of receptivity-closure is also a sly insult to our lover. We are essentially telling them, 'If you had any sense, you wouldn't be wasting your time with someone like me. Your attention would be better rewarded elsewhere.' Hold this attitude for long enough and it will become a self-fulfilling prophecy.

## Expectation & Receptivity

Our expectations wield a powerful influence over our receptivity aperture. If you are expecting your date tonight to suck, you will show up unreceptive towards your date. The coolness and distance your date perceives in you will raise their doubts and insecurities. They will think you dislike them at first sight. They will become less charming, more awkward. And voila, you will get your sucky date.

Bringing awareness into this dynamic between Expectation, Receptivity, Attitude & Result can be an eye-opener. This is a powerful mechanism by which we create a lot of our reality.

Between lovers, repairing the Receptivity between the two people often involves repairing the expectations between them. If you keep expecting your lover to fail with you, to disappoint you, then through your closed receptivity towards them, you will facilitate the unhappy outcome.

To live under the gloomy cloud of our partner's low opinion, expectation and receptivity is painful and demoralizing. When people are tempted to have affairs, what is appealing about the new person is that they are not relating to us from this dark place. They are interested in us; they find us worthwhile; they are receptive to us. They are holding the expectation that if they open up to us, they will have fun.

## Attention & Receptivity

The volume dial on these two factors tends to work in tandem. Increase one, and the other follows. Decrease one, and the other follows.

That which draws our attention, opens our receptivity. To find someone or something 'captivating' or 'intriguing' is to widen our receptivity towards them.

When we feel ourselves 'shutting down' to a person or an idea or a place, we want to retract our attention from said person, idea or place.

This is also a true but less understood phenomenon: That which you put attention on, you will become more receptive to! Even if in the beginning you did not find the object of your attention to be particularly interesting or attractive. The action and practice of directing your attention towards something will make you more receptive and susceptible to that something.

Within relationships, we are describing this phenomena whenever we say, 'He/She GREW on me.' The more you directed your attention towards that person, the more deeply you saw them. As a result, the more you found to like in them — to be receptive to.

When a relationship is in trouble, this attention-receptivity cycle has often stalled. Due to bad experiences and the build-up of resentment, the two people are no longer inclined to put attention on each other. The less attention they put on each other, the more their receptivity towards the other diminishes. Breaking through this diminished receptivity becomes a serious challenge. Any new attempt that one or the other might make to repair the relationship is not received by their partner. It's like pouring water on an overturned cup.

One of the exercises that therapists and coaches offer people at this point is this: Try to find *something* right in your partner, however small. Find the good that you can be receptive to. Focus on something worthwhile in your partner that you can appreciate, that you enjoy putting your attention on.

## Confidence & Receptivity

Confidence can be thought of in the above terms. To present oneself as confident is to make a tacit announcement, "I am worthy of your attention. Put your attention on me and you'll enjoy doing so. I am worth knowing. You are going to find it worthwhile to be receptive to me."

## Pride, Play & Receptivity

Pride is anchored in fear of Loss.
Play is anchored in Discovery.

Pride is concerned with the Self.
Play is focused on the other.

Defeat is a big deal for Pride.
Defeat is a shrug of the shoulder to Play.

Pride would prefer to win each and every time.
If Play won all the time, that would indicate that the game being played is too dull and simple. Play would make the game more difficult and essentially INJECT FAILURE into the Game to make it worth playing.

Pride & Play are not conventionally considered antonyms, but I find these two attitudes pitted against each other in our journey. There is a tug of war within each person between these two forces. And our Receptivity is linked to this struggle: The more we are in our pride, the lower our receptivity; the more playful we are, the greater our receptivity.

Pride seeks legacy.
Play seeks evolution.

Pride is efficient.
Play rambles and saunters.

Pride is moral.
Play is amoral.

Pride has no sense of humor.
Play is a trickster.

Pride is low receptivity.
Play is high receptivity.

Pride controls
Play surrenders.

## Permission & Receptivity

Have you felt freer with certain lovers and more constricted with others? What was it about these specific people that made you feel you could express yourself more openly, surrender more, let yourself be more vulnerable?

How much Permission do *you* bring to a lover? Do your lovers feel the Permission to express themselves emotionally and sexually around you? Is your 'permission field' an invitation for them to be more or less receptive?

We continually take our social and emotional cues from each other. To be civilized is to know how to act and present ourselves in the numerous social situations we encounter in life. Each of us knows how to act at a work meeting, or at church or with friends while watching a game, when out on a first date, or when at a midnight rave at Burning Man. We may not think in terms of 'Permission and Receptivity', but we are very much evaluating the level of permission for expression of our desires, our emotions and our eros in any given situation, around any given person. And we ourselves are communicating to others how they may or may not interact with us.

So, the level of permission that you bring to your relationships is a very important factor. Where greater permission is present, greater receptivity is possible.

Think of a lover, real or imagined, whom you might describe as 'wild'. Chances are, what made them wild was this permission-receptivity element. They were uninhabited and impulsive, impossible to shock, mischievous. Their Permission field was wide open and their Receptivity was wide open, and that created an invitation for you to also be uninhibited and self-expressed. If such a wild lover was also sane and stable, hopefully you held on to them.

## An Empty Cup

Want to give your lover the sexiest gift? Give them you as an empty cup. Do as much as you can to open up your Receptivity. Present your receptive self to your lover. It's hotter than lingerie and flowers.

Declutter your mind as much as you can before encountering your lover. Take care of your laundry lists or put them aside temporarily. Let go of as many of your resentments as you can. Try to repair any loss of trust that has occurred between you and your lover. Try to let go of past upsets and resentments.

Otherwise, all these will fill up your cup. They will clutter your field, make your mind noisy and reduce your receptivity.  And if your receptivity is low or missing, nothing will make up for it.  It won't matter how superlative your lover is, it won't even matter if you truly love them and find them very attractive.

Offer yourself as an empty cup.  That emptiness is a state of surrender through which Ecstasy flows.

— — — — — — — — — — — — — —

# 14. The Heart's Passage

There is a lot of talk of LOVE in this world. Let's not talk about Love here. Let's instead talk about our CONTAINER for love. We say our heart is where love resides. Our heart's location corresponds to the 4$^{th}$ center. When it comes to talking about love, the best I can offer you is my understanding of how this housing/container for love functions.

## Heart's Function

The heart's job is to break! The heart's function is to ache! To be heartbroken is the function of the 4$^{th}$ center! I know this sounds like a raw deal, but look at it this way —have you ever had any real choice in this matter? Has it ever been a real possibility to avoid heartbreak? It's not possible. Heartbreak, in all it's 1000 varieties, is what this 4$_{th}$ center is built for. It's how it grows. To be human is to be led on the path from heartbreak to heartbreak. It is an essential aspect of our human trek. It's how our soul grows. You could say this is actually the essence of our humanity; it's what the call of the human experience is. The finished human soul is one that has gone through and graduated from the tremendously painful and challenging experience of the heart's passage.

So understanding this passage, this evolution, can help us plunge into our journey with some courage instead of wasting eons trying to avoid that heart pain that constructs this 4th center — constructs a vessel robust enough to hold love, and allows passage to Ecstasy.

## Heartbreak vs. the Narrative of Heartbreak

There is a lot that passes for heartbreak but isn't quite it. It's very important to distinguish the central from the peripheral in the heart's journey.

Our stories of heartbreak aren't the true heartbreak. Our narrative sabotages the exquisiteness of our suffering. 'Stories of me' rob us of the genuine experience of longing, loving, losing, grieving, suffering. When we allow love/suffering to exist, to radiate through the 4th center, we have come to the door of heart's true journey; outside the door is the bright sun shining of Love. At this threshold to Love, we have the opportunity to raise our face up to the heat and light of the sun of love/suffering. If we stay there in that heat, the heart grows.

What we do most often is take a snapshot of the Love-sun, create a narrative out of our suffering, and then quickly pull down the shades. Because staying in that light of love/suffering is exquisite torture. So we take a snapshot of Love/Suffering and then we go around carrying a picture of that sun; we tell stories about how hot it is. We tell stories of suffering instead of simply suffering. We tell stories of lost love and broken hearts instead of sitting in the agony of our breaking heart. Suffering in real time and feeling that heartache in real time, in the present moment, is beautiful. It's excruciating, but it is also beautiful. It feels tremendously Here & Now when we are in the experience of it. The pain of it is indeed an EXPERIENCE, not a narrative that is seeking a resolution or an ending.

Heartbreak happens in present time. Compared to that, the narrative of suffering we construct is more like an artifact, a photograph — a THING instead of the PROCESS itself. And the *thing* of our story is always incomplete. It is limited by its perspective. It is limited by its editing—what we chose to include and exclude from our story, how we chose to frame and arrange the pieces of the 'story of me'. We carry that photograph around. It isn't anything real. But it is a good prop. It is an effective prop for sabotaging further experience. The artifact/narrative of past experience becomes an effective plug for keeping current and future experiences at bay.

Instead of opening the shade and exposing ourselves to the sun again, we walk up to the shaded window and tape our photograph of the sun on the closed shade. From then on, whenever life presents us with an opportunity to feel, to engage, to love, to let someone in, what we do instead is pull out our narrative-snapshot and tape it on the face of the present moment. We chose our old photograph over the human being who is in front of us. We cheapen life. We end up living a pretty impoverished and repetitive life. Instead of seeing the new experiences that are becoming available to us, we keep seeing the same narrative of suffering. Instead of opening ourselves to new heartache, we whine and carry on about the old heartache.

This old heartache is also one that we didn't let ourselves feel fully. That's the whole cleverness behind constructing the narrative. Our narrative is a mockery of experience. Our identity of 'oh-me-the-suffering-soul' is a mockery of true heartache.

A true experience of suffering, a true episode of forging in the 4ᵗʰ center, changes us a little each time. We come out of that fire a bit transformed. We may feel robust at first or fragile and tender, but that genuine suffering of the heart changes our soul, it shapes our inner container. Compared to that, when we are maintaining our narrative, we are eager to reshape all reality in order to keep our story and identity the same. We deny all change outside in order to remain unchanged ourselves.

In essence, NOTHING HAPPENS TO US when we inoculate ourselves from heartache. We essentially preclude experience; we preclude our journey when we resort to constructing camouflage for our heartache.

Life gives us many opportunities to let our heart be broken. Make yourself RECEPTIVE to the world and just about everything will start to break your heart. Let it! As much as possible. Let the ugliness of humanity break your heart. Let hate and prejudice break your heart. Let one act of kindness break your heart. Let one ecstatic touch break your heart. Let one experience of beauty break your heart. Let one experience of reverence break your heart. Let the magic of a million sensations that your body is capable of experiencing break your heart. Let the everyday miracle of walking upright down the street break your heart. Let yourself feel things. Let in other human beings. Let their longings and suffering break your heart. Let their pettiness break your heart. Let their rejection of your love break your heart. Let their yes and their no break your heart.

The art of the 4$^{th}$ center is to always be breaking instead of existing in a broken state. Let the breaking be ongoing. Let it be in immediate response to what is happening here and now. Let your heartache be fresh. Let it be current. Grieve now. Mourn now. Feel the loss now. Feel the humiliation and agony and discomfort now. Feel the graciousness and adoration now. Raise your arms up now, sing now, move now. Let your heart take in and commune with whatever is happening now.

## Sacrificing Humans to Our Narrative

To choose narrative over experience is also how we cravenly use other people as a means to our end. You can experience another human being only now. You can experience ANYTHING only now. When we choose narrative over experience, we use other human beings to buttress and decorate our narrative. Instead of a person we might let into our heart, we see one more way of rewriting our wounding and retracing our identity.

Don't use the human beings you encounter in your journey to keep feeding your narrative. This process also involves a great distortion of our perception; we don't really experience life as life is when we do this. We view the human beings who cross our path through heavily colored glasses of our narrative. We actually don't see others very clearly when we just use them to fortify our narrative. And this lack of seeing is a great unkindness.

From the wider perspective on the Heart's Passage, when you use others for your narrative, you deny their humanity; you humiliate them. By humiliating them, you become the heart challenge they need to undertake to forge their 4th center, to grow in Love.

From the soul perspective, to let others treat you as a means is better than to treat them as a means!

Let others deny your humanity rather than denying theirs.

Let them break your heart rather than vice versa.

And if you do end up breaking somebody's heart, if you do end up crushing them and humiliating them, then so be it! That's also fine in the big picture. We are here to humiliate each other. We are here to crush each other's heart and help each other forge the heart center so it may grow robust enough to hold Love.


## Narrative is the Sieve

There is a certain flip-flop that happens with our identity when we move deeper into our being. At a surface level, our narratives are very SUBSTANTIVE. At the level of our 1st and 3rd center of tribal and personal identity, our stories feel very real and actual. They have weight. They occupy a lot of space. They occupy so much space that they push out other possibilities. Our wounding and self-image hog the terrain of the 1st and 3rd centers.

But from the perspective of the 4th center, our narrative and identity look more like the holes in a sieve! Our identity actually constitutes our leakage! The more burdened we are with identity, the less sensation we are able to hold in our system. The more time-laden we are with the story of 'what has happened to me' the more quickly we leak present-time experiences out of our system. When we are too occupied with our narrative and wounding, we are literally not able to experience our experiences. We are not able to hold the new.

When it comes to sex and ecstasy, this sieve-like structure of the 4th center presents exactly the kind of challenge we would have if we were to try to FILL a colander! In this state of leaks and holes, we are not yet ready to contain ecstasy. Without forging our container in the heart's fire—without letting ourselves suffer in love and loss, we keep ourselves from forming the container to hold love and ecstasy.

If you've had a lover with such a container, you would observe that pleasure simply doesn't stay in their system. There is a momentary surge and then everything drains out. What's more, they don't seem to get nourished very deeply from affection and sex and intimacy. They may experience a momentary filling, but very quickly, certainly by the next day, there is no sign remaining in them of the pleasure, joy, ecstasy that they had inside of them a few hours earlier. Instead, the narrative of me has taken over once again.

# Heart's Passage is a Forge

Real suffering builds our soul. Allowing ourselves to truly feel and stay in the feeling of whatever is happening starts filling in the holes in our colander. Our heart becomes more and more robust. It builds CALIBER. It builds the strength and muscle and structural integrity to experience and hold genuine emotions. It becomes a truer vehicle for love and ecstasy.

The heart's passage is a forge. Many traditions, poets, and writers have said in one way or another that the heart is an organ of fire. The fire element has been widely associated with the heart or the 4th center. It is an on-spot description of what this center feels like when it is active. It feels like a burning. It feels like torment. It feels like punishment. But avoiding this punishment inevitably leads to a callowness of character. Those who avoid suffering in the heart at all costs in essence avoid loving at all costs. In modern lingo, we may say of such a person, 'they never make themselves vulnerable'. They never leave themselves open to hurt and wounding and getting kicked in the teeth. If you want to make fast progress in your heart center, try and get kicked in the teeth as often as possible. Love others, take chances, put yourself on the line, risk letting yourself be taken advantage of, risk rejection, risk dejection, risk heartbreak. Love's passage makes this risking of pain a prerequisite. To construct measures to avoid this pain is essentially cowardice — it's an indication of one's great fear of pain.


## Pride's Melting

PRIDE plays a big role in the heart's passage. Pride will keep you from taking that risk mentioned above. Pride wants to avoid failure. Pride dreads looking like a fool. Pride dreads declaring its love for someone and then having that person kick you in the gut. Pride is the cork that keeps energy from traveling up from the $3^{rd}$ center to the $4^{th}$.

Every spiritual tradition speaks of the virtue of HUMILITY. This is why! Pride has to be sacrificed for the heart to enter the forge. From the perspective of the $3^{rd}$ center, Pride feels like a strong, crystalline structure. It feels erect and complex and unyielding like a fortress wall. But from the perspective of the $4^{th}$ center, pride IS the holes in the colander of our inner container! Pride is an indication of where we are missing integrity, where we are porous, lacking strength for holding love and ecstasy.

Pride sabotages experience. It keeps us from evolving. To put yourself in the way of an ass-kicking requires humility. To let yourself be destroyed by loss and vulnerability and the pain of rejection IS what's needed for the heart to grow. Pride is a great impediment to those possibilities. It's very easy to see when you focus in on this equation: Can pride and devotion co-exist? Can pride and vulnerability co-exist? Pride and adoration? Pride and susceptibility? Pride and risking oneself in love? Pride is incompatible with all the various energies of the 4th center.

Pride is married to our old narrative. This may be a bizarre way to put it, but we are in fact PROUD of our wounding. Our wounding gives us a sense of self. It gives us an identity that is rooted in the past. Pride IS identity. And the heart's passage is a forge in which identity and pride are painfully melted down. And this melting down of our pride and identity feels nothing short of the experience of humiliation. It feels like a LESSENING of the self. The part that we had known thus far as ME feels smaller. And to get smaller in such a way, from the perspective of the 3rd center, is failure and death!

So if you want love, you can't fear humiliation. If you want love to grow in your life, make yourself humble in front of the bigness of love. Genuine loving WILL lead to humiliation! That's it! No humiliation, no love!

I'm not saying that this is ALL that loving brings. But this is one polarity of the 4th center. It will create painful humiliation at one end. And at the other end it will make Joy accessible to you. If you hang on to your Pride, you will not be able to touch the Joy that blooms in the 4th center. That joy pretty much grows on the ashes of pride.

## Humility's Strength

In this journey from Desolate Pride to Humble Joy is also the arc from fake strength to real strength. What takes more courage? Staying in Pride? Or letting yourself get humiliated? Pride looks strong. That's its whole front. But sacrificing pride takes more strength. Moving towards humility and humiliation takes real mettle. That's why just about everyone can do pride. Little children can do Pride. But moving forward in the heart's passage happens only after some wisdom and suffering has entered the soul.

There is something to be understood here also regarding false humbleness and true humility. Most of us choose to not ACT prideful. We don't want to be perceived as vain (or as pompous asses). So we may tone down our presentation and display a non-pride persona. But this is not any kind of true humility. This is merely cleverness and social navigation.

True humility is in owning one's pride and then wagering that pride so that it might get crushed. True humility is stepping up to do battle in your shiny armor and getting knocked on your ass in the mud. Real humility grows out from the pain of real humiliation.

## Humiliation Equation

The process of humiliation is pretty straightforward: Whoever loves more will be humiliated!

That's pretty much it.

Whoever is more openhearted will be humiliated. Whoever feels things more deeply will be humiliated.

In any relationship, we have the option of being more susceptible and receptive and thus being humiliated. Or we can be more self-protective, more prideful, more wrapped in our narrative and use the other person as a means to our end and thereby deny their humanity and their love and humiliate them instead.

Conventional wisdom will tell you to take the latter role —to be the non-vulnerable, non-humiliated party in any relationship. I'm prodding you towards the more masochistic choice. Get your teeth kicked in. For the heart is an organ of fire. If you are not in agony in your heart center on a continual basis, you have stalled the journey of the $4^{th}$ center.

## The Forged Soul

The character that results from this growth has real power in it. When one moves through the heart's passage, one becomes humble, but one does not become weak or a pushover. If anything, one grows into a genuine strength that others can perceive without us having to advertise it. No posturing is needed to convey that strength. The heart's passage is a true forging of our core. We are able to wield more energy thereafter. We become capable of feeling more within ourselves and giving more to others. Our inner capacity grows in volume and vigor with each forging episode.

The caliber that one builds with the heart's forging makes Ecstasy possible. This forging provides a passage for Ecstasy to rise and descend in our system. Ecstasy is scant possible when your heart is like a sieve. Nor is love possible. So that's the prize that awaits us for saying yes to the forge.

When glimpsing this love we may also finally gain some empathy for ourselves. We may appreciate just what a tremendous challenge this human experience is. We may feel a bit of kindness for ourselves for the sheer tonnage of loss and pain and self-loathing and humiliation that the human experience entails. We may finally look upon ourselves in our tremendous loneliness and feel compassion. It has taken tremendous courage to come on this human ride — to separate ourselves from our origin, to suffer, to fear death, to feel ourselves alone over and over, to perceive that we may be forsaken and abandoned by existence.

To reach this milestone in the heart's passage is to be halfway home.

## Narrative Is Fuel

Our Narrative is not the journey, but it can become the means for our journey. Burn the narrative! Use it as fuel.

Most of what passes as suffering in this world, the far and wide bulk of it, has NOTHING to do with the heart's passage. If you keep telling stories about what has happened to you, that's not it. If the suffering feels repetitive and stagnant, if you are suffering from the same heartache this year as you were last year, that's not it! If your suffering involves being angry and resentful at others, that's not it! All of that is just wounded pride and wounded identity and garden variety human tragedy that lives in our lower centers. If that's where you are, the heart's passage hasn't even begun.

The heart's fire has nothing to do with your history, your identity, your grievances. And in a way, all these varieties of suffering can become fuel for the heart's passage if you are ready to let them go as identity pieces and simply feel them and let them run through your system. Feel all the pain, all the love and lovelessness, all the loss, all the hurt. And do it in silence. The more you can hear yourself talking about your misery, the more you are not in your heart. The heart's passage is a solitary one. Forgive everyone who has hurt you and simply feel the hurt. That's what is called for.

Think of all your complaining and whining and miserable patterns as wooden logs that live in the lower three centers. These logs can be extracted from the lower 3 centers and tossed into the 4th center to build a really nice and potent fire. Build this fire in your heart and then burn in it.

The forging of the soul that results from this fire makes possible: joy, ecstasy, devotion, adoration, love, compassion, graciousness, peace.

## Higher Callings

It's also when this 4th center has reached a certain fortitude that one finally starts to feel that one is not entirely alone in this world. Up to the 3rd center we have no sense of any power beyond ourselves. People who never cross beyond the 3rd center will be prone to being atheists. They will be prone to the Nietzschean idea of Will to Power. Such people often reach prominent status in our society. They push themselves out into the world since their SELF is the greatest power that they know of. But on the flip side, people who are entirely undeveloped beyond the 3ʳᵈ center, people who are full of pride and absolutely dread vulnerability and humiliation also know very little of love. They are lonely at their core. And they are bereft of inspiration and originality—which descend down from higher centers.

Our demagogues fit this energetic and soul-profile.

Up to the third center, we understand only zero-sum games. To the 3ʳᵈ chakra warriors, taking the heart's passage is a sucker's deal. Letting yourself get humiliated is for losers. But this is the kind of loser you need to be to ignite the heart center. Many traditions speak of this transition point. They speak of humility. They speak of the last being first. They speak of the camel being able to pass through the eye of a needle before a proud man may enter the kingdom of heaven. They speak of the meek inheriting the earth. They speak of offering the other cheek. All these are propositions for suckers—when viewed from the pride of the 3ʳᵈ center. But such is the transition from the 3ʳᵈ to the 4ᵗʰ.

— — — — — — — — — — — — — —

# 15. ECSTASY

Ecstasy is tricky to talk about. In common speech and vocabulary, 'Ecstasy' may mean a lot of things and not much at all. It can be treated as a generically good state. 'Pleasure' is good; 'Ecstasy' is better.

My understanding of Ecstasy is more specific. It is specific and yet internal and invisible, so let me do the best I can to share with you what 'locale' of our consciousness and experience I am calling Ecstasy.

Imagine a ball of light the size of a cantaloupe. It is a lovely, bright, luminous, slightly buzzing ball of light—like a small, silver sun. It is mostly silver and 'light' in color, but if you continue to look at it you will see hues of every shade come and go on its surface. You will see a shimmer of pink and orange zip by along the silver, and then a veil of blue and purple.

Just being close to this little sun makes you feel centered in your soul. It makes you feel that you are not alone, that life is not random and cruel and brutish. That there is in fact tremendous order and beauty in the construction of the world. That EVERYTHING in human experience, the absolute worst of it—all of misery and hatred and pettiness and violence and cruelty—all of it actually fits. It's all ok.   All of it is a tremendous game.

At some level, we have built this game.  And at some level, the game has been built for us—for our journey, our expansion, even for our amusement!  Just being in the vicinity of this silver sun gives us all this—this sense of order and meaning and peace.  This silver sun is LOVE.

It's BIG love.  Cosmic love.  Godly love.  Love that transcends all relationships and all human context.

Imagine squeezing all of human experience as if it were a big basket of clean and wet laundry.   The water that you would squeeze out of every garment is the same water. That water is like love.  This simile falls far short of the real thing, but it will do.  Love is in the fabric of existence—or the blood force of existence.  If the fabric of existence were not imbued with love, there probably would be nothing here.  Or at the very least, there would be no life.  There certainly would be no such thing as an EXPERIENCE.

Well and good.  Love is the central, silver sun.

Now imagine a few smaller silver orbs in orbit around this orb of love. If the love orb is about the size of a cantaloupe in our model, imagine a few smaller silver spheres, maybe about the size of a peach or a plum, circling it. One of these plums is Ecstasy!

## The Artisans and the Astronomer

Imagine some of our earlier astronomers—the first curious souls who looked at the firmament with the suspicion that there might be more between heaven and earth than had thus far been accounted for in our philosophy. I imagine these first astronomers seeking to study and research, to seek real information, to be geeks! They went to the artisans in their towns and villages. They went to the glass blower and asked him whether he could fashion them a lens—something bigger and more pure in its shape and integrity than anything the glass blower might have crafted thus far. The astronomer went to the iron smith and the carpenter and gave them specifications for the construction of certain tubes and stands and gears.

The artisans might have been puzzled at first. 'What is this crazy person asking me to build? What will he do with such a contraption? We know how to make cabinets and vases and spectacles. Useful things! What is this nut job going to do with these odd pieces he wants us to craft?'

Imagine the astronomer gleefully constructing his new telescope and pointing it to the moon or to Mars and Saturn and seeing for the first time truths that others had not woken up to yet. We could say that the astronomer was having an EXPERIENCE that others had not gotten to yet.

Imagine the astronomer inviting over his artisans one clear night. He offers the glass blower and the carpenter and the ironsmith to look through the telescope so that they may know finally what he had done with the pieces that they had created for him. Imagine their thrill at seeing their artistry thus applied—to this end—to bring back a vision of the heaven that had thus far been missing from their cognition!

These bodies of ours are not so dissimilar from this analogy of the artisans and the astronomer. For most of our earthly existence, our bodies are an issue of contention and strife and struggle and mundane chores. We don't really know what it might be to BE who we are without our bodies. We don't know with certainty whether there is anything truly more to us than our bodies. And most days, this body is demanding and stubborn and prone to pain, hunger, fatigue, injury. Its vigor peaks early in life and then commences a slow, ignominious decline. It gives us days when being in our body is all but excruciating. Compared to that, on a good day, it at least permits us to go about our routine activities, to run our errands, to carry ourselves and our groceries home. It allows us to function in this demanding life and not be a burden to others.

But that's not all these bodies are. In our bodies there is also a heavenly possibility. Our body also has configurations that can be turned heavenwards. There are windows and doors hidden in here that open to startling vistas. There are passages in here that lead to old time and to giddy heights. The history of our origin is inscribed within these bodies. And there are immense trajectories waiting for us to lay claim to them.

Ecstasy is one such passage, one such trajectory that exists within. That is also us. That is also a configuration, an EXPERIENCE that is possible through the body. The body is the instrument of Ecstasy. It is anchored in our nerve endings and sinews. It is activated with breath and touch. It faces a 1000 obstacles. It seeks to rise and reach peaks that are our birthright to arrive upon.


## Ecstasy's Neighbors

Ecstasy is not the only plum-sized-planet that revolves around the sun of Love. There are other neighboring planets, other high frequencies of consciousness, that are part of this solar system. These include:


## BLISS

This is Buddha's Mona Lisa smile. Bliss is that high perch in the mountain peaks that great meditators touch from time to time. Bliss is very much a solo climb up the consciousness spectrum. Bliss isn't particularly interested in sex or the body or the other person. It is cleaner, less messy, more suited to the renunciate, the monk or the nun, the ascetic.

One reaches a very high point in one's awareness in Bliss where the dualities start to disappear — where the I start's melting into the Thou. Where the struggle of life that is built on polarity and strife tips its hand and shows you that it's all a game.

Most great traditions have sought the path of Bliss. Ecstasy has been too messy to grapple with down the ages. We've not been able to deal with our sex head-on and with clarity for about as long as we have kept our history. There may have been pockets of adventurous weirdos who sought to find god through sex, but they have always been scant in number and shunned by their neighbors.

Bliss is cleaner. It is less troublesome. It seeks to rise above the mundane. It has even been sought at the expense of the body. Punishing the body, fasting, abstaining from sexual pleasures and comforts, delicious foods and drinks have all been methods used by the Bliss seekers.

The etymology of Ecstasy translates as 'to stand out', as in to stand outside of one's body, to leave or escape the body. But the way I am using these words here, the experience of *Bliss* is more an experience that is Out of the Body. Bliss aims to leave the body behind and have the consciousness itself rise to a great height. Ecstasy, as used here, is very much ANCHORED in the body. It is anchored in our sex and our skin and our genitals and every erogenous zone. In our breath and sound. In somatic experience. Ecstasy rises up from the body but remains rooted in the corporeal.

## DEVOTION

This is another great path that many beautiful traditions have employed. It is a heart-based path of great power. Within Christianity, those who feel a greater affinity towards the Holy Mother follow the devotion path. Sufis very much approach the divine through the path of love and devotion — God as the beloved.

Within the Hindu tradition, devotion is just about everywhere. There can be great warmth and softness in the devotional approach to the divine and the higher spheres. Like Bliss, Devotional paths also generally bypass our erotic aspect. The Devotional path is about the relationship between oneself and the divine. The Ecstasy that I am talking about is reached through the relating of two of our very human, mortal and flawed bodies.

## ADORATION

This is a close cousin of Devotion. You might almost consider Adoration a moon of Devotion in this orbital system of consciousness. Adoration evokes gratitude, graciousness, abundance, hopefulness in us. 'Let us adore Him', it says even in a Christmas carol. In the Hindu tradition, Krishna evokes the path of Adoration. In Christian sermons, when the preacher prompts the congregation towards 'Amen', 'Praise Jesus', 'Thank you Lord', 'Blessed be Thy Name', these are all prompts for us to rise heavenwards in gratitude and adoration of the divine.

Adoration makes for a particularly powerful path in group experiences and worship. So much of great religious music and chanting is inspired through this channel of Adoring God, Praising God, reaching up to the heavens with our voice and instruments and declarations. Adoration is a bit more human and humble compared to Bliss.

Adoration seems to say, here I am — down here on earth — gravity bound and in difficulty and challenged and imperfect. But I know it's within me to REACH heavenwards. While keeping my feet on the ground, I know I can reach grace if I cultivate graciousness in my heart, if I thank god for the life I have been given, if I sing and call and extend heavenward, I can touch the rays of the divine.

## Suggestions for Interacting with Ecstasy

Don't try to live there!

To touch Ecstasy is plenty. To float in it for a few minutes is beatitude. Ecstasy doesn't lend itself to clinging in any case. If you are inclined towards acquiring and possessing and keeping, Ecstasy will elude you. Don't try to take Ecstasy in your fist. Let IT lift you. Imagine that Ecstasy decides whether you visit it or not. You can't really get there by will and force. There is much you can do to prepare yourself for Ecstasy, yet no amount of preparation will grant you a straight and reliable passport up to Ecstasy. Stay humble. Stay available. Be gracious when you are able to touch it. Let your self and your life be nourished by it. And then let it go.

## The Obstacles Are the Point!!!

There are many obstacles on the path. Confronting our obstacles, taking them on, looking into them, grappling with them—all that emotional, relational, spiritual drudgery IS THE POINT! We are not meant to bypass our obstacles and sneak our way to Ecstasy. Moving on the path and encountering all that is blocking our way is the real journey; it's the human journey.

This is why I consider this messy, sticky, body-bound, people-bound, relationship-bound path towards the higher frequencies of consciousness one of the richest and most essential.

The mess of relationships is why we are here! To be human is to endure and grapple with human relationships. To me, any path to the divine carved outside of human relating is ultimately lacking and incomplete. All those seekers who are escaping the misery and the mess of human relationship and seeking the divine INSTEAD, are in for a surprise down the road. This kind of detour is not really permitted in the long journey.

So plunge in and deal with the mess. Relate! Encounter humans fully. Actually take on the long-delayed journey of fully stepping into your sex with awareness, and see if even through this rickety and colorful vehicle of human relations, you are able to touch Ecstasy together with another.

## Solo Ecstasy?

We are great believers in self-reliance these days. This is a point of ego you will find in many spiritual seekers as well—they will propose that they don't need the other to find their way to the divine. That they ALONE, by the virtue of their pure and stalwart character, can make their journey to the mountain peaks. I believe them. I know its possible. But it's not the same journey!

Imagine being in good physical shape and running 10 miles on a straight, paved road through the desert. That's certainly an accomplishment! Well done! You have indeed shown you have strength and stamina.

But now imagine having to gain 10 miles of ground in trench warfare! People are trying to kill you from every side. The terrain keeps changing. You don't know who to trust or what's going on half the time. Sometimes when you think you have made progress, you realize you've only made a loop and ended up where you were yesterday. That's human relationships! Finding ecstasy through you own body, all by yourself, is also wonderful. But it is a narrow and simple path compared to touching Ecstasy with another human being.

Our intimate relationships are the great tests of our lives. As with our bodies, our relationships are fraught with indignities and embarrassments and errors and fatigue. Which is as it should be. We are here to take on the obstacles that the human experience contains. None of that is to be avoided. The invitation here is to also turn our instrument heavenwards from time to time. That realm up there is also ours to claim.

— — — — — — — — — — — — —

# EPILOGUE

# EPILOGUE

# We Don't Have A Sexual Culture

This may sound like an odd statement to make. The people of our planet collectively spend an ungodly sum of money on pornography every year. Sex is used to sell everything on the shelf. It certainly seems that we are inundated in sexuality—from our billboards to our magazine covers to television. Offers of sex for money are also always near at hand. But I stand by this premise: We don't have a sexual culture.

This commodification of sex is in fact a big symptom of the absence of real sexual culture among us. If we had real sexual culture, it would NOT belong so heavily to the realm of commerce.

## Commercial Appropriation of Sex from a Chakra Perspective

Commerce belongs to the 1st center.

Sex lives in the 2nd center.

In the commodification of Eros, the 1st center has appropriated the 2nd center. We have lowered the possibilities in sex by tethering it so firmly to money and material gain.

Ecstatic Sex becomes possible when the energy of the $2^{nd}$ center is allowed to rise up to the $4^{th}$, $5^{th}$ $6^{th}$, and $7^{th}$ centers.

If sex were just left alone and not meddled with, it would flow naturally and thrive in the $2^{nd}$ center first. This would look like 'normal' sexuality. On our planet today, perhaps only some remaining primitive/aboriginal cultures might display this normal functioning of the $2^{nd}$ center. This would have to be a tribe with no particular indoctrination against Eros. One or the other sex would not be considered inferior or evil because of their sex. Sex is basically left alone among these people. It follows a mostly biological path. It is mostly procreative. It is acknowledged and enjoyed openly and even communally as all other pleasant aspects of life.

Eros in this primitive culture would be a normal topic of discussion and exploration. Sex would not be hidden away. People would not pretend that sex did not exist or attach a strong sense of privacy to it. Adults would not be obsessed with protecting young members of society from sex. Sex would be talked about. Sexual experiences and discoveries would be shared openly among the people same as other knowledge and stories are shared among the people.

That would be normal 2nd center functioning.

What we have on the vast majority of the planet—in the more liberated western countries as well as the more repressed areas—is NOT this normal functioning of the 2nd center. We have the commodification of sex. By the standards of most of the world, this normal functioning of the 2nd center in the isolated tribe would be considered terribly permissive and promiscuous and uninhibited.

## The Gnarled Tree of Eros

Imagine planting seedlings for a variety of trees that generally grow up to be high and stately trees. Imagine planting some oak trees, some sycamores and willows. We shall plant them in healthy and fertile soil. We shall give them plenty of water and sunlight. Only, we shall put an impregnable glass plate over them about 5 feet off the ground. What do you think will happen to these trees? What would happen to the saplings as they grow higher and hit that immovable glass plate?

The spidery and twisted mess that the growth of those trees would take is the state of our Eros on the planet today. One can't really destroy sexual energy as such. One can try suppressing it. We can put obstructions in the way of that energy, forcing it to redirect itself and twist in on itself. The result of such obstruction is what we have in the world today. The commercial culture of sex that we live in is the gnarled and tortured tree of our Eros that has not been permitted its natural growth.

## Sexiness Good. Sex Bad.

This combination is one of the odd consequence of the gnarled tree of Eros. In the more repressed areas of the world, both sexiness as well as sex are shunned. But on the rest of the planet, this statement stands. Sexiness is coveted, while sex is feared and ostracized. The entire commercial empire of sex stands on this premise of Sexiness Good/Sex Bad.

In perfume and fashion ads it is plain to see that they are of course not selling SEX; they are selling Sexiness.

I would propose to you that the entire juggernaut of pornography is also not selling sex. Pornography sells sexiness.

What is sexiness? Sexiness is the salacious report of sexual pleasure. Sexiness is the promise of Ecstasy. Sexiness is an image or hologram of what one does not have, of what is missing from one's life. Sexiness is a thought, an idea, a proposition. It is an enticing invitation that you have no way of accepting. It is incorporeal. It cannot be held or touched or embraced. Sexiness can never be had. The purpose of sexiness is to stir up the pool of our repressed eros. Sexiness is a gust of wind blowing through our tortured and gnarled tree of Eros.

Sexiness is saltwater. It does not quench our thirst. It is not meant to. It is deception. It is designed to appropriate our action, our motivation, our money towards its own directed ends. It is saltwater masquerading as the promise of pure water that may actually bring us satiation.

## True Eros

What would sexiness be in a culture in which sex was not bad? What would Sexiness Good/Sex Good look like?

That would look like Erotic artistry.

Imagine the Erotic equivalent of a concert hall full of enthusiastic music lovers listening to a great performance and delighting in it. Imagine the Erotic equivalent of a group of friends meeting together, relishing each other's company and sharing a sumptuous meal that they have cooked together. Imagine the Erotic equivalent of a bunch of neighbors gathering together to work on a community garden and then delighting in the blossoms that come in Springtime as a result of their collective effort.

It's probably difficult for most of us to imagine exactly WHAT the Erotic equivalent of such expression and communal experience and delight would be. We haven't experienced them!

If that tree of Eros were allowed to grow naturally, if it were allowed to rise to its natural height and expanse, then we would have true Erotic culture. And it would yield the same level of art and genius as any of our other passions which are allowed to thrive openly and are allowed to grow a culture around themselves.

## We Are Tantalus.

In the meantime, we are like the cursed Greek hero, forever condemned to a state of craving. We get the verb 'to tantalize' from his predicament. Tantalus was punished by being made to stand in a pool of water beneath a fruit tree with low hanging branches. But when he would reach up to take the fruit, the branches would rise out of his grasp, and when he would reach to drink from the pool, the pool would recede from him.

That is also our own experience of the commodification of sex that is all around us. We live constantly in the promise of sexual joy and ecstasy. We live in craving. We live in dissatisfaction.

## Our Capacity for HAVING has Diminished.

This is one very odd and tragic scenario that comes my way on a regular basis. I counsel a couple where one of the partners (usually the man) seems more interested in pornography than in connection and sensuality with his flesh and blood woman. The common hypothesis for this preference for images over a real body is that the man has habituated to the extreme sex between the extreme bodies that he has been absorbing through pornography, and real sex simply can't measure up to that.

There is probably some reality to this premise. But I don't think it's the whole story. It may not even be the predominant factor that is at play. This premise makes an equivalence between 'Porn Sex' & 'Real Sex'. I think this premise is incorrect. As discussed above, porn isn't sex at all.

Considering porn to be a category of sex is like considering images of food to be a category of cuisine.

If a person has been 'feeding' themselves off an image collection of delicious looking food, what relation does that visual bingeing have to do with actually putting real food in one's mouth?

In a culture where the predominant engagement with our Eros takes the form of craving and longing, our capacity to EXPERIENCE sex has gravely diminished. Our ability to stay present during sex has atrophied! Simply put, we are checked-out during sex most of the time. Real sex, physical touch, and a rise in erotic sensation, when it happens, is novel and confronting for a vast majority of people. Our capacity for HAVING sensation has diminished as a result of the absence of real sexual culture. It isn't so much that Porn Sex is trumping Real Sex. It's that porn sex has atrophied people's capacity for real sex and human connection. The longer we stay in the land of craving, the more our capacity for having will diminish.